I0413902

INEQUALITY TENSION AND CONFLICT

INEQUALITY TENSION AND CONFLICT

Canice Chucks Osuji

Copyright © 2018 by Canice Chucks Osuji.

ISBN: Softcover   978-1-5434-9038-1
               eBook   978-1-5434-9037-4

All rights reserved. No part of this book may be reproduced or transmitted in any form or by any means, electronic or mechanical, including photocopying, recording, or by any information storage and retrieval system, without permission in writing from the copyright owner.

This is a work of fiction. Names, characters, places and incidents either are the product of the author's imagination or are used fictitiously, and any resemblance to any actual persons, living or dead, events, or locales is entirely coincidental.

Any people depicted in stock imagery provided by Getty Images are models, and such images are being used for illustrative purposes only.
Certain stock imagery © Getty Images.

Print information available on the last page.

Rev. date: 08/03/2018

To order additional copies of this book, contact:
Xlibris
800-056-3182
www.Xlibrispublishing.co.uk
Orders@Xlibrispublishing.co.uk
772995

This book is dedicated to all people around the globe who are victims of inequality.

ACKNOWLEDGEMENTS

Many thanks to my family, friends, and other well-wishers.

Great thanks also to Mr Banfur, who helped in proofreading of this work.

Also to share in my gratitude is Nwadibia Chiamaka for reading through this work.

Thanks to J. Hopman, a Catholic priest in the Netherlands, for his assistance in the early part of this work, and Gregory Robinson, a worthy friend from the Dominican Republic. I equally appreciate the efforts of many who, in one way or the other, made this project a reality. Finally, the most wonderful appreciation goes to the life-giver Jehovah, who has been watching over my soul.

FOREWORD

Our world today is characterised by many vices, which make it seem a place of anguish and pain. This is so because one race, tribe, or group is always struggling to overthrow the other. Most times in order to do this, they employ all forms of negative mechanisms to pull the other down in order that they may stay on top.

On seeing the title of the book, one would think that in discussing inequality, the author would meander into the deliberations on issues like robbery, prostitution, and other common sociopolitical problems that oftentimes are brought about by inequality. But no, the issues touched in the book, I must acknowledge, wouldn't be more appreciated than now when our society is at the mercy of marginalisation and unexplainable discrimination. The author, no doubt, did an exhibition on the problems that have eaten deep into the roots of our society, exposing how much damage has been caused already.

In our society today and around the world, where one cannot simply stay without the fear of domination, the author reveals how bad the menace of inequality has become, hence appealing to human conscience for all to turn a new leaf and safeguard the human future. This he did from meaningful research that has given birth to this wealth of knowledge. Since one of man's responsibilities on earth is to make the world a better place, this book becomes a veritable asset to achieving that. The book seeks to bring to bear the wounds and havoc man has inflicted on the society and suggests the remedy or the ways to heal the wounds.

Furthermore, this book will help the reader to understand that inequality has its forms, and they include racism, social stratification, discrimination, and marginalisation. The author provides so many examples to explain what inequality means. This is without mentioning countries and instances where it is practiced in the said countries. There is no doubt whatsoever that the reader and all men who wish to make the world a better place will find this book quite impressive.

Nwadibia Chiamaka
Imo State, Nigeria

CONTENTS

INTRODUCTION

The lack of equal and fair treatments for all in the global scale have been fuelling resentments, hatred, dissection, unwarranted tension, including terrorism. However, scholars of different schools of thought may argue that inequality has been in existence since the creation of the world or existence of man. But we are now living in a global and more integrated society, where human rights, laws, and conventions stand against lack of equal opportunity and treatment for all. From generation to generation, inequality has become part of human problem that needs to be addressed if we want to live in a world void of tension and conflict.

There is a biblical cum philosophical injunction that says that we should treat others the way we would like to be treated or do to others the way you want them to do unto you. Jesus Christ also said that we should love our neighbours as we love ourselves (Mark 12:13). It is also said that he who saves one man has saved a whole human race, but he who destroys a man has destroyed a whole human race.

These are basic principles that should rule the minds and hearts of each and every one of us, but unfortunately, human beings have failed to accept these. Some say that inequality is making the whole world sick. Mohandas Gandhi of India said, 'Nothing belongs to any Indian unless millions of Indians who cannot afford a plate of chapatti are fed.' But today India is at the center of inequality in many areas of the society, where caste system and racism have eaten into the society as a cankerworm eats into the fabric of clothes.

One may ask what inequality is. It means lack of equality, or imbalanced treatment of persons. In law, equity means that everyone is equal before the law; that means we all should be handled in the law court without prejudice, preference, or favour.

Today, equality before the law does not really exist, since

- Some are above the law.
- Some are treated more favourably and kindly than others. The quest for justice has eluded present-day society.
- Some have risen above the law because of unequal application of the law, unevenness in many areas, or imbalanced treatment among persons.

This does occur when other races, tribes, classes, status, religion, communities, or nationalities are involved. Inequality can also be defined as lack of equality in an instance, difference or variation in size, amount, rank, quantity, social position, an unevenness on surface, lack of proper proportion, unequal distribution, etc. We can as well define inequality as disparity, irregularity, dissimilarity, contrast, difference, favoritism, and imbalance.

Today, many still have reasons or opinions that empower them to treat people unequally, irrespective of the call by all for equality. People can testify from generations past that we have seen inequality being practiced in every government and private organisation of our society. Even in our individual homes, inequality can also be seen. For instance, it is possible to find ourselves hating one child and loving the other. Also among brothers and sisters, inequality can also be noticed, especially where one brother has stronger ties with a particular one of his brothers than with the rest, though this type of inequality does not generate tension, hatred, or conflict; this is because it is part of human nature to co-exist in such an imbalance. We are, rather, concerned with a different type of inequality that creates division as well as tension and conflict around the globe.

We are living in a different era, where technology has increased the level of awareness. This makes the practice of inequality with its associated ills more obvious than before. The advent of live media coverage as well as the Internet has widened human society's idea of newsgathering. So news that can take years or months before people can be aware of it can now be heard and seen around the world within a space of hours, if not minutes. Therefore, the cry and yell for equality in many areas or all walks of life need to be addressed to reduce global conflict and tension. However, the cry for equality should not be a mere outcry without solution in sight. It is also a fact that many who do cry for equality fail to treat others equally. In most cases, equality is theoretical and practically it has eluded human society.

Inequality can take the form of imbalanced treatment between the rich and the poor. This type of inequality is the oldest and most fatal ailment of all republics, according to Plutarch. However, the imbalance that exists today exceeds that of the rich and the poor but it cuts across many areas: imbalanced treatment and favoritism of race, tribe, religion, one country against another, one gender against another, class, etc. Inequality comes in the form of discriminatory attitude going contrary to established norms and rules.

All republics or states around the globe have, in one way or another, adopted systems that inherently have the idea of inequality in order to limit or hinder other rival groups from ascending in political positions. There is a general overview that inequality appears in all activities of mankind or governments around the world. It is evident that this problem cannot be completely overlooked because it is the agent of all tension and conflict we have seen in human history and continue to see today.

Because of the pain we feel when we are treated unequally, some tend to go the extra mile to address inequality through agitation. Sometimes when our voices are not heard, we tend to go beyond verbal. This is when it turns ugly; people or groups of people might take up arms as an alternative. All conflicts and tension around the globe are for demanding equal and fair treatment and integration. Inequality always finds a way to alienate.

Thomas Carlyle said, 'A man willing to work, but unable to find work is perhaps the saddest sight that fortunes of inequality exhibits under the sun.' Carlyle went further to say, 'We all know that while the law of competition may be hard for individual, it is best for the race, because it insures the survival of the fittest in every department.' We therefore accept and welcome it as a condition to accommodate ourselves.

Andrew Carnegie (1835–1919), in his opinion about inequality, said, 'Greater inequality of environment, the concentration of businesses or industrial and commercial activity in the hands of the few and the law of competition between these, as being not only beneficial, but essential to the future progress of the race.'

George Bernard Shaw said, 'Idiots are always in favour of inequality of income because it is their only chance to eminence.'

The disease of inequality is infectious, since all republics and sectors of the society have seen it as the only way forward in order that their own world, race, tribe, religion, class, gender, and nationality might dominate and harshly take advantage of others. As a result, we cannot hesitate to ask if inequality is making us sick. Do we all have equal chance to health, education, income, employment, political power, and socio-economic opportunity present today in our so-called integrated and globalised world? The answer is a capital NO, since the practice and acceptance of unequal treatment to many has the potential of benefiting the ones who have advantage. Many will continue to support, oppose inequality, and agitate for equal and fair treatment for all, irrespective of the mindset of those who cherish inequality.

However, it has to be clear to all politicians and policymakers that so long as inequality thrives in our society, tension, conflict, and terrorism will never be reduced or come to an end. When tension and conflict end in one part of the globe, there is the tendency these will continue in another; the circle of violence will be continued. We all therefore have to work collectively in all honesty to address this menace and disease of mankind in order that we may have a better world with limited tension and conflict.

CHAPTER 1

Gender Inequality

First and foremost, *gender* refers to the attributes and opportunities associated with being male and female, the relationship between women and men, girls and boys. These attributes, opportunities, and relationships are socially constructed and learned through socialisation processes. They are contextual or time specific and are changeable. Gender determines what is expected of a woman or man in a given situation. In most societies, there are different responsibilities assigned to women and men. These responsibilities usually project the idea of inequality.

In most cases, the inequality takes different forms but includes activities undertaken, access to and control over resources, and decision-making opportunities. Gender is part of broader sociocultural issues such as class, poverty, and so on.

The full realisation of democracy requires the participation of all citizens on equal terms, with a balanced representation of men and women in the economy, decision-making, and culture of the people. During the last few centuries, considerable progress towards racial, gender, ethnic, and religious equality has been achieved in the world, especially in North America, Western Europe, Africa, Asia, the Middle East, and Oceania. However, we are still a long way from reaching full equality between races, tribes, religions, and between men and women in their day-to-day lives.

Facts indicate gender inequality between men and women still exists. Let us remember what the musician Peter Tosh once said in his album *Equal Rights*: 'Everybody is crying out for peace; I want no peace, what I want is equal right and justice, that's what I want, man.' Since equal rights, justice, and peace are related, we can assume that if all are treated equally and justice is highly applied without some being above the law, peace will automatically be achieved. It is factual to say that when all are treated with justice, equity, and fairness, tension, bickering, and conflict are not the order of the day. Remove the chains of oppression and yoke of injustice, and the oppressed will go free. One way to do this is by sharing your food with the hungry and opening your homes to the homeless poor. Give clothes to those who have nothing to wear, and do not refuse to help your relatives (Isaiah 5:4–6). You may not be a believer, but I believe our world needs a society devoid of tension and conflict.

Over the centuries, men and women have fought hard for equal opportunities and treatment regarding gender inequality. In a world dominated by men, women have always been relegated to the background in the sociopolitical activities of the society. The British Sex Disqualification (Removal) Act of 1919 ended the exclusion of women from various official positions in Britain.

However, gender is constructed both socially through social interactions as well as biologically through chromosomes, brain structure, and hormonal differences. The dichotomous nature of gender leads to the creation of inequality that manifests in numerous areas of human life. There is no problem seeing and taking note of gender differences, but when we use gender discrimination to limit people from exploring their full potential, it becomes a problem that needs to be addressed.

SEXISM AND DISCRIMINATION

> Gender inequality can be understood through sexism.
> In order to be exploited, they are viewed in relation
> to the warmth they can provide and as incompetent.
> (*Wikipedia*, 'Gender Inequality')

This brings us to another concept: benevolence sexism. Benevolence sexism takes place when women are viewed as possessing low degrees of competence and high degrees of warmth. Benevolence sexism is a stereotype against women. It contributes to gender inequality as it is only applied to women who conform. The concept also plays to the idea women are weak and in need of men's protection.

This brings to mind the concept of hostile sexism. Hostile sexism takes place when women are viewed as having high levels of competency but low degrees of warmth. This form of sexism is framed as an antagonistic attitude towards women and is always associated with the ideology that women attempt to control men through sexual seduction or feminist ideology.

> We see related discrimination in networking business.
> Men are getting hired more often or are being promoted
> thus discriminating women due to taste or preference
> for other men because they share similar characteristics.
> (*Wikipedia*, 'Gender Inequality')

EQUAL PAY FOR WOMEN

This regards pay inequality between men and women. It is often introduced into domestic politics in many first world countries as economic problems that need government regulation. In third world countries, because of cultural and/or religious reasons, pay disparity is generally much higher. During the 2007–2008 US presidential election campaign, candidates promised equal pay for equal work for men and women without disparity. It was yet to be implemented in the administration of President Barack Obama.

For years, many across the globe have campaigned for equal pay for men and women. Yet we still live in a world where unequal pay continues to thrive. Though there has been improvement over the years, more needs to be done to reduce this type of inequality. In countries like Japan, pay inequality has become history; it leads other countries in equal pay for men and women. In England, it has been proven that even in the twenty-first century, unequal pay between men and women continues. It is confirmed that even regarding executive bonuses, women still receive 80 per cent less than their male counterparts in the same field or office.

GLOBAL GENDER PAY

The report commissioned by the International Trade Union Confederation in 2008 shows clearly that based on their survey of sixty-three countries, there is significant gender pay gap on the average of 15.6 per cent, meaning women earn, on average, 84 per cent of men's earnings. Women who are engaged in work in the informal economy have not been included in these figures. Overall, figures for gender pay gap throughout the world range from 13 per cent to 23 per cent. This report argues that even higher education of women does not necessarily lead to a higher pay gap over their male counterpart. It also argues that this gender pay gap is not due to lack of training or expertise on the part of women, since the pay gap in EU member states increases with age, years of service, and education.

Gender Inequality in the Workplace:
Income Disparity Linked to Job Stratification

Wage discrimination is the discrepancy of wages between two groups due to a bias towards or against a specific trait with all other characteristics of both groups being equivalent. In the case of gender inequality, wage discrimination exists between the male and female gender. Historically, gender inequality has favoured men relative to similar qualified women. (*Wikipedia*, 'Gender Inequality')

Once factors such as experience, education, occupation, and other job-relevant characteristics are taken into account, 41 per cent of the male-female wage gap remains unexplained. As such, considerations of occupational segregation and human capital theories are not enough to understand the continued existence of a gendered income disparity. The glass ceiling effect is also considered a possible contributor to the gender wage gap or income disparity.

This effect suggests that gender provides significant disadvantages towards the top job hierarchy, which becomes worse as a person's career goes on. (*Wikipedia*, 'Gender Inequality')

The gender gap also appears to have narrowed considerably beginning in the mid-Sixties, when some 5 per cent of first-year students in professional programs were female. By 1965, this number jumped to 40 per cent in law and medicine, and over 30 per cent in dentistry and business schools. Before the highly effective birth control pill was available, women planning professional careers which require a long-term, expensive commitment had to 'pay the penalty of abstinence or cope with considerable uncertainty regarding pregnancy'. Taking control over their reproductive decisions allowed women to move easily and make long-term decisions about educational and professional opportunities.

Additionally, with the reliable birth control pill, young men and women had more reason to delay marriage. This meant the marriage market available to any woman who 'delayed marriage to pursue career . . . would not be as depleted'. Thus, the pill could have influenced women's careers, college majors, professional degrees, and marital age.

Gender Inequality in the Home:
Gender Roles in Parenting and Marriage

Gender roles develop through internalisation and identification during childhood. Sigmund Freud suggests that biological signs based around the penis determine gender identity through identification with either the mother or father. While some people agree with Freud, others argue that the development of the gendered self is not completely determined by biology based around one's relationship to the penis but rather, the interactions one has with primary caregivers. From birth, parents interact differently with children depending on their sex. Through this interaction, parents instil different values or traits in their children based on what is normative for their sex. This internalisation of gender norms can be seen, for example, in the types of toys children are typically given. 'Feminine' toys often reinforce interaction, nurturing, and closeness. 'Masculine' toys reinforce independence and competitiveness. Education also plays an integral role in the creation of gender norms.

> Gender roles created in childhood are spread throughout life and helps structure parenting and marriage, especially outside the home and in work. (*International Journal of Educational Administration and Policy Studies*, http://www.academicjournals.org/IJEAPS).

Inequality against Women in Elections:
Adult Suffrage

Over the centuries, women around the world have been limited by the power of male-dominated political culture, where women are not allowed to participate equally in political activities, such as policymaking. It has been proven that elections are a primary source of injustice and inequality against women as well as against minorities in many republics throughout history. Men have been given greater power to vote and to be voted for in electoral processes, while women are given a secondary role, though we all say we are practicing democracy.

Though democracy demands equal participation of all citizens of a given state, this has not been the case as regards women around the globe. These biases, which especially discriminate against women, need to be corrected so that women can realise or demonstrate their full potential in the areas of politics and governance. Many of the so-called states of modern democracy and those who claim to be models to be emulated have failed to address and rectify this issue.

For over 232 years of American independence, their leaders seems to have sworn that it will take a long, long time for a woman to rule America. In addition, Britain has said that it will take a long time before a woman can occupy No. 10 Downing Street after Margaret Thatcher.

If you do not believe it, the democratic world, such as the US and UK, are allegedly bringing liberty, democracy, and equal opportunity to the so-called undemocratic states around the world. So it is also good to ask: Does the concept of democracy, liberty, and equal opportunity also extend to American women? Why is it that in 232 years of American independence, not even one woman has become the president of the United States of America?

Even Great Britain, which for the centuries has prided herself as the host of the mother of parliaments, only one woman, Mrs Thatcher of the pigeons of Trafalgar Square fame, has become prime minister of Britain. Looking at the current positions of the two parties, I can bet that it would not be possible in the near future for a woman to rule Britain. Information reveals that women over 21 have been able to vote in parliamentary election in England since 1928. Can you imagine, as recently as 1928? Can you imagine that? Even as recently as 1928. Some women have been eligible since 1918, but voting was limited to women who were over 30 years of age and who were either householders or the wives of householders. The link between the rights to vote and owning property or land also applied to men. In fact, men over 21 years generally were only given the vote in 1918. Nevertheless, before that, men had to own property or pay rent over a certain limit and as recently as 1911, the electoral registers list contains only 60 per cent of all men over 21 years in the English population. In the 1800s, rules were yet stricter, and only men who were landowners qualified. In practice, this meant that only the richest people voted. They were able to keep control of their wealth and have a large influence on the local and national politics. This, in fact, does not tell the full story about the hard struggle that British women went through to get the right to vote.

> The move for (British) women to have the right to vote had really started in 1897 when Millicent Fawcett founded the National Union of Women's Suffrage. Suffrage means the right to vote and that is what women wanted—hence its inclusion in Fawcett's title. However, Fawcett's progress was very slow (as she believed in peaceful protest). She converted some of the members of the Labour representation committee. (*History Learning Site*, 'Suffragettes')

Thus, Britain and Europe were plunged into world war on 1 August 1914. In a display of patriotism, Emmeline Pankhurst instructed the suffragettes to stop their campaign of violence and support in every way its war effort. The work done by British women in the First World War was vital. In 1918, the representation of the People's Act was passed by Parliament, which partially gave the right to some women to vote. Those who were given the right to vote were those over 30 years old and who were either householders or the wives of householders.

Today, the descendants of these men who sat on the democratic rights of their women for centuries come all out in verbal and written attack on the less-developed countries, preaching the virtues of democracy, liberty, and equal opportunity. In some cases, they put sanctions on others for failing to conduct themselves democratically, while their own women are still kept away from the post of president or the prime minister. We have also, to acknowledge the work done by both men and women in recent years, to promote equal opportunity for women in the political arena. It is of paramount importance that women are giving more or equal slots in our society in every area so that they can participate on equal footing with the opposite sex, the men.

From this story and others alike, we see how the fight for equal treatment can get out of hand if not properly managed. Tension and conflict can arise when inequality is ignored by those in power and policymakers. Women by their nature are more peaceful than men, but when they turn violent, we will not but interpret it as the result of their neglect. All index points show that inequality cannot be allowed to continue without solution if we want to reduce tension and conflict of any nature. I do not think that Emily Wilding Davison would be so happy to have wasted her talent and education if the inequality meted against her gender was addressed by those in authority.

WOMEN'S SUFFRAGE

Women's suffrage refers to the economic and political reform movement aimed at extending suffrage, the right for women to vote and be voted for, in order to hold public office. The modern origin of the movement was in France in the eighteenth century. Of currently existing independent countries, New Zealand was the first to give women the right to vote, in 1893. Similarly, the colony of South Australia enacted legislation giving women the vote in 1894. The places with similar status which granted women the right to vote include Wyoming Territory (USA), 1869. Other possible contenders for first 'country' to grant female suffrage include the Corsican Republic, Isle of Man (1881), Pitcairn Island, Franceville, and Tavolara, but some of these had brief existences as independent states while others were not clearly independent. Australia extended this right in 1901 to some women, and then in 1902 to all non-Aboriginal women. With this attitude, Australia still practiced inequality against the Aboriginal women. The first independent nation to grant suffrage to women would be Sweden, where some women were in fact allowed to vote during the Age of Liberty (1718–1771), although this right was far from applying to women in general.

Voting right for women was introduced into international law in 1948, when the UN adopted the Universal Declaration of Human Rights.

As stated in Article 21

1. Everyone has the right to take part in the government of his country directly or through freely chosen representatives.
2. The will of the people shall be the basis of authority of government.
3. This shall be expressed periodically by genuine elections, which shall be by universal and equal suffrage and shall be held by secret vote and by equivalent free voting procedures.

Women's suffrage is also explicitly stated as a right under the convention on the Elimination of All Forms of Discrimination Against Women, adopted in 1979.

HISTORY OF SUFFRAGE

Women's suffrage has been granted at various times in various countries throughout the world. In many countries, women's suffrage was granted before universal suffrage, so women from certain races and classes were still unable to vote. (*Ballotpedia*, 'Women's suffrage')

Suffrages were extended to Norwegian women in 1913 and Denmark also, other countries followed suit: British women over 30 years old in 1918, Dutch women in 1918, American women in 1920, Turkey in 1926, and in 1928, all British women were given the right to vote on the same terms with men. It was extended for persons over 21 years. One of the most recent jurisdictions to grant women full equal voting rights was Bhutan in 2008. In 1935, eighteen female MPs joined the Turkish parliament. However, we still have places where women's suffrage is denied or conditioned such as in

Brunei: Women (and men) have been denied the right to vote or stand for a legislative election since 1962.

Lebanon: Partial suffrage. Proof of elementary education is required for women while voting is compulsory for men.

Saudi Arabia: No suffrage for women. The first local elections ever held in the country occurred in 2005. Women were not given the right to vote or to stand for election, although suffrage may have been granted by 2009.

United Arab Emirates: It is limited, but it will be fully expanded by 2010.

Vatican City: No suffrage for women—while most men in the Holy City also lack the vote, all persons with suffrage in papal conclaves (the cardinals) are male.

SUFFRAGE MOVEMENT

The suffrage movement was a very broad one which encompassed women and men with a very broad range of views. One major division, especially in Britain was between suffragettes who sought to create change constitutionally and suffragettes who were more militant. There was also a diversity of views on woman's place. Some who campaigned for women's suffrage who felt that women are naturally kinder, gentler, and more concerned about children. It was often assumed that women voters would have a civilising effect on politics and would tend to support controls on alcohol, for example. They believed that although a woman's place was in the home, she should be able to influence laws which will be of impact upon that home. Other campaigners felt that men and women should be equal in every way and that there was no such thing as woman's 'natural role'. There were also differences in opinion about other voters. Some campaigners felt that all adults were entitled to a vote, whether rich or poor, male or female, and regardless of race. Others saw women's suffrage as a way of cancelling out the votes of lower class or non-white men. The most current ongoing movement for women's suffrage is in Saudi Arabia. The issue branches into the complicated role of modern Saudi women.

SUFFRAGETTES' BRUTAL TREATMENT AT OCCOQUAN WORKHOUSE

5 NOVEMBER 1917

Alice Paul led the more radical wing of those who were working for women's suffrage in 1917. Paul had taken part in more militant suffrage activity in England, including hunger strikes that were met with imprisonment and brutal force-feeding method. She believed that by bringing such militant tactics to America, the public's sympathy would be turned towards those who protested for women's suffrage, and the vote for women would be accepted finally after seven decades of activism.

And so, Alice Paul, Lucy Burns, and others separated in America from the National American Woman Suffrage Association (NAWSA, headed by Carrie Chapman Catt) and formed the Congressional Union for Women Suffrage (CU), which in 1917 transformed itself into the National Woman's Party (NWP).

While many of the activists in the NAWSA turned during World War I either to pacifism or to support of America's war effort, the National Women's Party continued to focus on winning the vote for women. During wartime, they planned and carried out a campaign to pike the White House in Washington, DC. The reaction was, as in Britain, strong and swift and led to the arrest of the pikers and their imprisonment. Some were transferred to an abandoned workhouse located at Occoquan, Virginia. There, the women staged hunger strikes, and as in Britain, they were force-fed brutally and otherwise treated violently under orders from W. H. Whitaker, superintendent of the Occoquan workhouse, as many as forty guards with clubs went on a rampage, brutalising thirty-three failed suffragettes.

They beat Lucy Burns, chained her hands to the cell bars above her head, and left her there for the night. The hurled Dora Lewis into a dark cell, smashed her head against an iron bed, and knobbed her out. Her cellmate Alice Cosu, who believed Mrs Lewis was dead, suffered a heart attack. According to affidavits sworn at that time, other women were grabbed, dragged, and beaten, choked, slammed, punched, and kicked.

Tension and conflict can be avoided or reduced if we all can in a collective and honest way address inequality in whatever form or wherever it exists. Naturally, when our cries for equal treatment are neglected, the possibility of tension becomes imminent. When verbal demands are made for equality, those who benefit from inequality tend to treat it with disregard, to the disfavour of those who are victims. As this attitude lingers, there is no other alternative than to speak in a violent way, since they say that action speaks louder than voice.

MANY FACES OF GENDER INEQUALITY

Once, Nobel laureate Amartya Sen observed how gender inequality also plays in the household. He saw the household not as an undifferentiated unit, but as a unit of cooperation as well as inequality and internal discrimination. Also, he had a critical look at the many faces of gender inequality, mostly in South Asia. In the census data of 2001, there is evidence of profound gender inequality and therefore there is a need for action to combat and put to an end the inequality in this part of the world and other areas where it exists.

Here let us use South Asia, especially India, as a case study to understand what we mean by many faces of gender inequality.

REFLECTING ON SOUTH ASIA

It is pertinent to take note of the variety of forms that gender inequality can take. First, inequality between women and men cannot be confronted and overcome by any one set of all-purpose remedy. Secondly, over time the same country can move from one type of gender inequality to harbouring other forms of that inequality. There is evidence that India is undergoing such a transformation right at this time. Thirdly, the different forms of gender inequality can impose diverse adversities on the lives of men and boys, in addition to those of women and girls. In understanding the different aspects of the evil of gender inequality, we have to look beyond the predicament of women and examine the problems created for men as well by the asymmetric treatment of women. The casual connections which illustrate this can be very significant and can vary with the forms of gender inequality. Finally, inequalities of different kinds can also frequently enough feed each other and we have to be aware of their interlinkages.

Though we are concerned here with gender inequality in South Asia, or the Indian subcontinent, let us not think that the United States or Western Europe and other places such as Africa and the Middle East, are free from gender bias simply because some of the empirical generalisations that can be made about the subcontinent would not hold in the West. Given the many faces of gender inequality, much would depend on which face we look at.

For example, we know that India along with Bangladesh, Pakistan, and Sri Lanka, has had female heads of government, while the United States or Japan has not yet had and does not seem very likely to have in the immediate future. Indeed, in the case of Bangladesh, where both the prime minister and the leader of the opposition are women, one might begin to wonder whether any man could possibly rise to a leadership position there in the near future. Another example shows that as early as 1960 at the University of Delhi, there were more women professors than at Harvard University in the 1990s, or presently at Trinity College of Cambridge.

REFLECTING ON AFRICA

Despite the 1979 Convention on the Elimination of All Forms of Discrimination Against Women (CEDAW), the 1995 Beijing Fourth World Conference on Women and the 2003 Maputo Protocol to the African Charter on the Rights of Women in Africa: attaining the full rights of women in Sub-Saharan Africa has been an uphill climb against patriarchy, poverty, and autocracy. A combination of problems faced by women results from the fact that they are underrated, misunderstood, and placed as second-class citizens. Women have little or no say in policymaking processes that directly affect their lives. In times of war and conflict, they are victimised and violated. They are subject to human trafficking especially in regions like Sub-Saharan Africa, Eastern Europe, and Asia. They experience the worst form of violence: gender mutilation. By and large, they are reduced to a state of powerlessness and vulnerability. Women are marginalised economically and culturally viewed as inferior.

However, they vastly contribute to economic production and development, whether it is by working on the fields, participating in microfinance activities, peacemaking, or nurturing children. In most African countries, men dominate the political landscape as women are relegated to submissive participation by intimidating cultural beliefs, myths, and attitudes. Though women are quite visible on the election campaign trails adding life, colour, and numbers, they are barely visible when it comes to the front seat of politics and representation.

The election of Mrs Johnson as the president of Liberia has shown that women can bring hope and peace to the continent of Africa if given the chance to participate fully in the political process. Also, Mrs Dora Akunyili was the head of Nigeria Agency for Drugs and Counterfeit Control. NAFDAC is the organ that fights against abuse and use of both illicit and fake drugs in that country. She was able to work strongly and effectively to limit flow of fake and illicit drugs into Nigeria. This also proves that women can even do better in governance in Africa than the men when given the chance. There were many assassination attempts on her life by the bigwigs and criminals, but that did not deter her from getting the job done. The result is there to prove that in the recent years, she has done the best job in this area of fighting crime in that country Nigeria.

Also, people like Martha Karua have featured prominently on Kenya's political scene for a good seventeen years. She has been described as principled, eloquent, arrogant, tough and abrasive, a hardliner, litigious, tactless, and a troubleshooter. That is a lot of things for one woman, and there is still more. Arguably, she is one of the most powerful women in Kenya, tagged the iron lady of Kenya politics. In 1999, she was named jurist of the year, but most remember her for boldly walking out on President Arap Moi, who was at the time addressing a rally in Kirinyaga District. She has actively championed for the widening of democratic space and gender issues in the Republic of Kenya. She has been a leading crusader for the rights of women through public interest litigation, lobbying, and advocacy for laws that enhance and protect their rights through her work with outstanding women's organisations like the International Federation of Women's Lawyers (FIDA-Kenya) and League of Kenya Women Voters. By virtue of her role as the Minister of Justice, National Cohesion, and Constitutional Affairs, she has been at the centre of key reforms outlined by the national dialogue and reconciliation process overseen by chief mediator Kofi Annan during the last election stalemate in Kenya.

People like her and other well-spirited women of Africa should be allowed in leadership in the continent than continue to leave our political leadership in the hands of men such as Kibaki, Odinga, Obasanjo, Mugabe, Kaddafi, and their like. They say what a man can do, a woman can do better. Let's give the women of every society the chance they deserve; maybe we can have a better world order.

CHAPTER 2

Racial Inequality

Different racial and ethnic groups are unequal in power, resources, prestige, and presumed worth. The basic reason is power. Power is derived from superior numbers, technology, weapons, property, or economic resources. Those holding superior power in a society—presumably the majority group—constitute inequality by dominating less-powerful groups. This system of inequality is then maintained and perpetuated through social forces. However, it does not actually mean that those who dominate racially or ethnically are always the majority in population per se. Cases abound where the minority race or ethnic group takes over the majority and dominates them over time.

It has been shown throughout history that there is a significant relation between race and inequality, and this has created tension and known conflict around the world. The idea of one race or ethnic group claiming superiority against others has been the genesis of the inequality, racism, and related ills emanating from supremacy of one race against another. To many who believe in God Almighty and to those who do not believe, the Bible tells us that God created human beings. He created them male and female and not with a specific colour. But today, men have created colour as a basis to propagate their own goal in order to dominate or take advantage of others

Europeans have been in the forefront of racial/ethnic bias and unequal treatment of others who seem different from them. Centuries ago, they migrated to different continents looking for food and shelter. By the time they are welcome to a place, they will automatically turn against the natives, take control of the people as well as their lands. Finally with warlike nature that is peculiar to all wanderers, they will make war and destroy the inhabitants of the host land. They will dominate people and treat them unequally. This is no new concept and is just a fact well known to many around the world because many are their victims, from Africa to Australia, Asia to America, and the Middle East as well. Inequality associated with race and ethnicity has limited many from reaching their full potential around the world. The issue of racial/ethnic inequality as well as other forms of inequality has been the major factor contributing to violence, tension/conflict, and terrorism.

A RACIST WORLD

Charles Darwin in 1839 said that when two races meet with each other, they behave like two animal sort, they fight and eat each other up. This is Darwin's opinion which he and his like even till today use to promote racism in our world. People have used difference in races to create room for inequality, which leads to tension and conflict around the world. This has been predominant among the Aryan race. Though among different groups of people, there has been an element of distinction, even among people of the race be it Aryan, black or coloured. But the use of race to divide and create tension among people has been promoted by the Aryan race.

However, throughout history, men have neglected and humiliated others who look different from them. The differences can be religion, race, class, social status, sex, issue of body structure, colour of the skin, difference in the manner of dressing, or supporters of different sport clubs.

Racism comes from manifested angry feelings, hatred, or humiliating others who look different from us. It can be someone's different character and possibly decided through the body group in which people belong. We know that somebody cannot change his/her birth. Through this, men have their eyes set on the person in a racist manner that limits his chance of education or self-development or aspiration. Racists think their own race is superior to the other races or ethnic groups. They find it justified, therefore, to belittle and treat others with less respect and unequally. They discriminate and insult, as well as mishandle them in areas of life.

Through racism, people have been denied equal opportunity in the field of education, occupation/work, medical care by resulting daily humiliation and sometimes systematic killings such as genocides, slave trade, ethnic cleansing via gas chambers. Mostly Europeans have been the architect of racism against others such as Africans, Asians, and Arabs; however, white people are the only ones that have the idea of being a superior race on the ground of their colour. Far before that, the Arabs had such an attitude before they were defeated in many battles by Europeans. Between AD 630 and 708 when the Arabs invaded the African continent, they considered themselves even superior to Africans. In many regions around the world, some ethnic groups consider themselves superior to others and therefore take control over them, be it in Africa, Asia, Europe, the Americas, etc. Some Japanese tribes still believe that they belong to a race superior to other Asians, such as Koreans and Chinese.

Yet white racism has lasted more than any other feeling of superiority of one race against the other. Both in Europe and North America, racism persists till to date in every area of life. Though they claim to be Christians, they still refuse to accept the biblical word that God created all men equal, male and female he created them, not black and white or red and coloured (Genesis 1:26–27). Even the Declaration of Independence of the United States of 1776 said that all men are born or created equal. However, many still refuse to accept these principles but propagate that they are 'more equal' or superior to others, especially the black people, their main target.

At the beginning of the nineteenth and twentieth century, most white people saw themselves as superior to Africans, Asians, Arabs and other ethnic groups and even their host in North America (Native Americans). Through the control of power by the West and rule over many, the whites believed they had conquered the world. Their achievement in science, war, and technology, medicine gave them riches. Through these as well as colonial expedition, they acquired other people's resources from other continents, which gave them power other groups had no access to. But, they forgot that Greeks looked down on them in the earlier centuries when they were been ruled by them. History shows that before the West made achievement in the areas of medicine.

Imhotep of Egypt was the world's first medical doctor. He was the world's first known architect who built the first Egyptian pyramid. Till today, Western science is still amazed with the Egyptian system of preserving the dead (embalming or mummification). Even after knowing the truth about Imhotep (2630–2611 BC), Western scientists still supported the idea of Darwin in order to spread their racist agenda, published in 1859, *The Origin of Species*, where they claimed superiority to other races. They claimed that inferior races such as blacks are closer to monkeys than they are, using the survival of the fittest as a basis of being the strongest species and therefore they have the power to control others. The blacks were primitive while the whites were civilised, but they forgot that civilisation started in Africa (Egypt). Even the British prime minister Arthur Balfour, 1902–1906, of the Conservative party said that it is absurd to believe that Africans and whites are in any way equal or from the same human being. However, if there are black monkeys, we have now seen that there are white monkeys too.

RACISM AND RIGHTS

By 1900, racism within science did develop into a complex system. There began to exist different ways of thinking about relations between humans. Democrats, liberals, and socialists began to think in terms of human rights, equality, and universal brotherhood. Knowledgeable scientists, liberals and socialist scholars began bringing the idea of individual freedom and equality irrespective of colour, race, or belief into human society. Christians also learned that every man has a soul and is valuable before God. It was Christian liberal ideas that brought slavery to an end, though some Christians had allowed and permitted slavery beforehand. At the beginning of 1900, almost all of Western society had accepted Jews slaving among them after centuries of discrimination. However, the discrimination of the West against the black people and other minorities around the world continued. In the beginning of the twentieth century, many in the West had started to fight and struggle against white superiority (supremacy), using the Western idea of human rights and Christian ideals to fight racism. This helped to alleviate and reduce the degree of violence and hatred meted against others by Aryan nationalists and their agents.

On many occasions, you get confused with the compassion of the white people and the degree of violence they used against non-white people. Many a time, their compassionate attitudes are so benevolent that you appreciate everything about them. On the other hand, when you read the history of their occupations and colonial regimes of atrocities, you begin to wonder where their compassion has gone.

COLONIALISM

In 1907, the then future British prime minister Winston Churchill said that Africans were under the influence of British authority and instruction and their back position should come to an end. But it is a well-known fact that history textbooks published in 1911 in Britain for children under the age of 13 years contain derogatory and racist text about black people. These children read that blacks in the West Indies are lazy, unkind, and aggressive and are not in a position to improve or work unless they are forced to do so. They also taught the children that blacks (including those in the West Indies) are always happy but worthless and spend their income only on nice and good clothing.

At the beginning of the twentieth century, most African countries and the West Indies were under the control of the Europeans. Britain had the greatest empire, followed by France, the Netherlands, Germany, Spain, Portugal, and Belgium. All had important colonies. Most of these colonies were a result of people conquered by the Europeans in wars, some of which lasted for 300 years, but most of them were conquered in the second half of the nineteenth century.

All the European colonial governments were at least democratic by the Europeans' acclaimed standard of the knowledge of the people to choose their leaders. But the natives whom they ruled had no real political rights. The colonialists denied the natives their rights because they claimed superiority of civilisation. So in this context, they did not respect the principles of democracy, since there was no equal participation of all citizens of the land. The white Europeans said that they had to control land and the people's resources because the blacks and non-white people (Asians, Arabs) were not in a position or state to manage their own affairs. However, they forgot that these people have been running their own affairs before the advent of the white man. They also failed to recognize the historic realities of the old, ancient civilisations of Africa, India, and China. I remember Marco Polo from Italy was the first to bring paper money to Europe from China. In the book *The Growth of Civilization*, W. J. Perry noted that the mode of government of ancient Egypt was in all probability carried out by means of councils. But to the West today, Africans are people who are unable and incapable of managing their own affairs or rule themselves.

There are Europeans who were honest witnesses to the true story in Africa before the advent of the white man, some of them merchants and travellers who wrote unbiased accounts on Africa's civilisation of Guinea Coast days. Filippo Pigafetta's *History of the Kingdom of Congo* was published in 1591 and stated that the circumference of the kingdom was 1,695 miles divided into six administrative provinces. The people were a swarming crowd dressed in silk and velvet, well-ordered and down to earth in the most minutest (sic) details. They had powerful rulers, flourishing industries civilised to the marrows of their bones.

In the Gulf of Guinea, 'the European captains of ships were astonished to find streets well laid out, bordered on either side for several leagues by two rows of trees. For days they travelled in a country of magnificent fields inhabited by men clad in richly coloured garments of their own weaving.'

In the recent centuries, the European colonialist has swept this part of African history under the carpet and depicts Africans as people who are dumb, stupid, uncivilised, unintelligent, and incapable of ruling themselves or managing their own affairs. Before they abandoned the colonies in Africa and other places, they left government in the hands of Africans they trained with their racist and discriminating attitude to rule the continents. They sowed the seed of tribal, ethnic tension and conflict among peace-loving brothers who now turn against themselves in wars with the weapons of the West. The Europeans said that they taught us how to read and write, but today, a book has been discovered in Mali which is up to 500 years old, written by Africans in their own language. It is not up to 300 years since the West came to take over Africa as its colony.

I would advise all the Europeans who know less about the black man's history or African history to go and read about the experience of an Englishman on his visit to the Ashanti kingdom, now Ghana, in 1817. Bowditch expressed his view and what he saw during the great procession in Kumasi of the king's retinue in 1817.

Schoolbooks, newspapers, and romance in Europe propagated their colonisation of Africa, Asia, and the Middle East as a subject of superiority. They called the people of African descent cannibals and mysterious, evil creatures who therefore should be killed. With all these theories, they formulate literature for their children about Africans. The white artists made themselves happy with arts of primitive Africans and Polynesians. The irony about all these is that the Europeans were also raping all these Africans whom they depict as evil, mysterious creatures and cannibals. In 1911, the French *Le Petit Journal* showed a picture of how the French were bringing civilisation to an uncivilised North Africa.

On 13 April 1919 in the town of Amritsar in Punjab during a demonstration by Indians against the British colonial government in India, the British general Dyer ordered the shooting of protesters, and about 379 of them were killed, including children and women. Later the British queen bestowed the honour of 'Sir' to General Dyer for his crime against humanity in India. In the then Kenya (Africa), the British government and her soldiers castrated many of the Mau-Mau members who stood against the British Empire. Despite the crimes and racist atrocities committed by the Europeans, the colonialist still present themselves as helpers rather than oppressors, for example in Madagascar.

In all practicality, the colonial rule was a racist administration wherever it occurred, except somehow the French, who practiced the policy of assimilation. The whites lived exceptionally good lives in many areas during the colonial era. The natives were not allowed access to the white areas, except those with special privileges. They applied the divide-and-rule system by choosing some minorities whom they liked over the majority tribes or ethnic groups. People who were living together for ages were turned into enemies overnight by the white government everywhere they found themselves.

Colonialism came to an end due to the experience the West had during World War II, which undermined their economy and colonial power. The Japanese defeating the Europeans in Asia in 1914 let white people know that they did not have the monopoly of power and that non-whites can defeat them in war. The Europeans lost their trust or hope in their felt God-given mission to rule over and control other people. The rise of educated elites in the continent of Africa also propelled Africans to fight for political independence from the West, which really paid off in political freedom in a way since they were still under the control of the West economically.

FASCISM AND INEQUALITY

In the early 1920s, 1930s, till the late 1950s, many countries such as Italy, Germany, Spain, Japan, Portugal, and Hungary came under the leadership of military dictators and government. These governments became known as fascists, among whom are Mussolini of Italy, General Franco of Spain, Adolf Hitler, and others. They see their own people as superior to others, thereby using it as a basis for discrimination and racism. They justify conquering others whom they say are inferior.

Benito Mussolini, Italian dictator, came to power in 1922 and was a typical example of humiliating others who are not Europeans as inferior. In 1935, he attacked the only independent country of Africa, Ethiopia. His army used poison gas and bombs against Emperor Haile Selassie's empire. They also attacked Japan in 1931. They attacked Manchuria and in 1937 took over a large part of China. Propagandists of fascists described the Japanese as a superior race that was destined to rule Asia.

Without a doubt, the German National Socialists (Nazis) under Adolf Hitler were the most fanatic racists' regime in history. In 1914, during World War I, Germany was defeated and fell into economic chaos, and Hitler claimed it was caused by the Jews. He had the most racist theory where he claimed that the Aryan race of blue-eyed Germans and Scandinavians by nature are a superior race; other races were slaves. He also rejected the idea of intermarriage between Aryan race and non-Aryan race. But he himself did not have blue eyes, though many dumb people followed and accepted his theory. He wanted to destroy all non-Aryans and then have unified control of his government over others.

In his book *Mein Kampf* in 1925, he said that the Nazi party didn't believe in equality of race. He believed that men have the obligation to believe that a better and stronger race has to win over or control an inferior and weaker race. In 1933, German newspapers preached propaganda, how Jews in Germany, France, the USA, and England were locked outside. German anti-Semites were all the time racially profiling the Jews on newspapers. The Nazi party claimed that Jewish bankers and communist Russia were working together in order to control the world and its economy. They created racist tension and unequal treatment against Jews and other races. Hitler considered Jews as tumour/cancer, an evil that had to be removed from the Aryan German society.

Sometimes you wonder if Europe and the rest of the world are not going to witness another political agenda similar to Hitler's. When you see today in football fields around Europe, her citizens continue to chant racist chants against black players, you worry and think that

Hitler is still alive and well in Europe. Even those whose families were victims of the Nazi ideals today join fascist and Hitler supremacy clubs promoting racism and hatred. In fact, many in Europe still need to be re-educated about history and events of the past.

ANTI-SEMITISM

There has been a long tradition of hatred of the Europeans towards the Jews in Europe for centuries that continues till date. In Central and Eastern Europe, such as the Ukraine, Hungary, and Poland, the big Jewish communities have always been seen as enemies. During the First World War, great numbers of Jews were killed. In fascist Hungary, the people were forced to hate the Jews and gypsies (gitanos). Many Jews tried to leave Catholic Poland, who saw them as enemies.

In the First World War, Jews in England fought for the English, German Jews for the Germans, and French Jews for the French. By the 1920s–1930s, the fascist movement came to England and France, and they began attacking Jews and their businesses. Oswald Mosley, leader of the British fascists' union blamed the Jews and other races for unemployment and economic chaos in England.

On 9 November 1938, Kristallnacht, tens of thousands of Jews were rounded up and sent to concentration camps. Their shops and synagogues were attacked and set on fire. Britain and the USA protested Hitler's action but refused to accept the Jews who were trying to escape from Germany to be admitted into their respective countries.

RACE AND INEQUALITY IN THE UNITED STATES OF AMERICA

In the United States and around the world, there is in inequality between different groups of people. But the United States as the world superpower and leader of democratic principle is taken here to be a case study with regards to its application of equality and respect to democratic rules. The United States has failed in fulfilling the foundation laid by the founding fathers that all men are born or created equal and should be treated as such (Declaration of Independence of 1776).

The idea that there is significant correlation between race and inequality is not a new concept. Some dispute that race is overemphasised, but historical evidence suggests that the unequal treatment of racial minorities in the United States dates as far back as the start of colonisation. In the early days of settlement, Anglo-Saxons encountered a group of people who appeared racially different from them. American Indians were discriminated against because their beliefs and practices seemed savage to the European visitors. However, let us not forget that when the Europeans arrived by the 1620s, the Native Americans did not see them as savage. The natives accommodated them in their land and taught them how to grow crops. It was when the Anglo-Saxons became rich in the land that the Native Americans became inferior, primitive, and therefore a target of discrimination and destruction.

Rather than colour or racial distinction, religious and ethnocentric criteria were used initially to separate groups into superior and inferior categories. The pattern of discrimination continued with black–white relations when early Americans (Europeans) implemented the institution of slavery. Although there were plenty of resources in early America, settlers needed labour power to fully utilise the land. Forced labour was common during this time, but the prolonged use of Native Americans or indentured white servants seemed impractical. Importing non-white slave labour from Africa became their most viable and attractive option. Slaves were imported and traded for over two long centuries in the United States. Europeans raided African towns, cities and forcefully carted away the children of Africa.

Other minority groups have also been discriminated against in the United States. Latin Americans, Asian Americans, and people of Middle Eastern descent have also been subjected to racial discrimination, stereotype, and unequal treatment. Asian Americans are unlike other minorities in that they are considered a model minority. This is because they have succeeded in education, upward mobility, income, and avoiding the criminal justice system despite being discriminated against. In any case, these patterns of discrimination against minority groups have resulted in a society with significant racial inequality. This disparity exists in many forms and institutions, including

Income and wealth
Education
Health
The criminal justice system
Access to property / property rights.

INCOME AND WEALTH

Income refers to a flow of resources over time and represents the value of labour in the contemporary labour market and the value of social assistance and pensions. It is a valuable gauge of economic inequality. The income of racial minorities has increased with reduction of racial discrimination in the labour market. As a result, the hourly wage gap between minorities and whites has narrowed. While this suggests that the various races are competing in somewhat level playing field, it is challenged when wealth is taken into account.

Income is what the average American family uses to reproduce daily existence in the form of shelter, food, clothing, and other necessities. In contrast, wealth is the storehouse of resources; it is what families own and use to reproduce income. Dating to the inception of slavery, a governmental policy prohibits blacks from beginning businesses. The Federal Housing Authority made it difficult for African Americans to obtain loans and mortgages. While racial and ethnic minorities were legally denied opportunities to accumulate wealth for future generations, most whites did not encounter these same obstacles. Perpetuations of these practices for centuries attested to the wide wealth inequalities among whites and minorities, especially blacks.

Because home ownership plays such a large role in wealth portfolios of American families, it is a prime source of the differences between black and white net worth. Home ownership rates for blacks are 20 per cent lower than rates for whites, hence blacks possess less of this important source of equity.

In 'The Hidden Cost of Being African American', Thomas Shapiro uses the concept of transformative assets to explain racial inequality in wealth. Transformative assets are inherited wealth from previous generations that lift families beyond their own achievements. Inheritance is important right now because the generation that benefited from post–World War II economic boom is now at the age when they are passing on their wealth to their children. In his research, Shapiro finds that these assets help white people more than they help African Americans. White people have more wealth and head-start assets than African Americans do. This, according to Shapiro, is the crucial cause of the disparity between African Americans and whites with regards to wealth because inheritance is the key determinant in what kind of life families can enjoy. A disparity in wealth between African Americans and whites exists even when there are similarities in economic achievements such as income, level of education completed, and job quality. There is also a wealth gap between blacks and whites of similar incomes, similar levels of education, and similar job quality. In all comparisons, black families have less wealth than white families.

Housing is a very important component of the personal wealth. In the United States, home equity makes up 44 per cent of people's net worth. According to Shapiro, wealth built up in one's home is by far the most important financial reserve for middle-class families. African Americans are at a disadvantage because they are unable to get the same quality of housing as whites do. While explicit segregation does not occur anymore, it is still more difficult for African Americans to purchase a good-quality home. These are several factors that explain why this imbalance in transformative assets has led to racial inequality between blacks and whites.

First, whites have less debt when they are ready to settle down because they are more likely to have gotten assistance from their parents for their college expenses. Secondly, it is common for banks to grant lower interest rates on mortgages for those who can put a higher down payment on a home. Many white families rely on transformative assets to make these down payments. African Americans, on the other hand, generally do not have the same access to these assets and rely on their own savings instead. Therefore, it is harder for black Americans to make higher deposit on a home, thus making it more difficult to obtain a low-interest mortgage. Thirdly, communities that have higher percentages of African Americans are more likely to suffer from a loss of property value because of the perception among white people is that black Americans drive down property values. Banks practice redlining and choice of which areas are good for investments, which disadvantages African Americans because primarily black communities are considered to be bad investments.

Because of this perception, white flight occurs when there is an influx of black Americans into a community, thus creating a system of de facto segregation. This segregation is maintained by the perception from whites that an influx of black Americans would lower property values and increase crime. However, this fact is also true in England and many European countries and even in non-white lands where whites find themselves. It is like in their nature, they find it difficult to cohabit with black people but sometimes they are happiest among blacks.

A huge implication of this segregation of communities that results from wealth is inequality in education. Housing discrimination and the effects of transformative assets limit educational progress. Communities with better home values receive more funding for schools. This results in better-quality schools in primarily white suburban communities, while primarily African American and Hispanic communities in the inner cities do not receive adequate funding or government attention.

Owing to the ever-growing gap between white and black Americans are their weekly earnings. In 1981, black males averaged a weekly income that was approximately 20 per cent below that of white males. Furthermore, not only do black males not get paid the same as white males, they are also more likely to experience unemployment. In 1980, black males on average were over 60 per cent more likely to endure unemployment than whites. Also, their time in unemployment is 30 per cent longer than that of white males.

These statistical numbers are also not expected to change any time soon. Research showed that from the years 1948 to 1974, the racial income gap was closing at an annual rate of 0.4 per cent. Many studies have shown that earnings do not increase with job experience for black males as they do for white males. These studies have also shown that black males get hired for jobs that have few promotional benefits. On the other hand, white male accept jobs with training requirements to receive promotions and pay raises. In brief, white males receive jobs with promotional incentives and blacks simply do not. These statistical findings illustrate the ever-large discriminatory state the United States is in. Black males on average still receive 40 per cent lower wages a week than that of whites, even if they have the same schoolings and job experience. In 1960, white males made $700 more than blacks if both had less than elementary-level education. Furthermore, blacks were paid on average $1,400 less than whites if both had a high school diploma. These statistics rise even higher if both received a college degree; whites were paid $3,800 more than blacks.

In today's society, minorities are labelled before they are even known. Distinct groups such as black males and Hispanics are branded in a condescending fashion before they open their mouth. Race is socially constructed, and because of this, minorities do not receive the same opportunities to succeed in society that their white counterparts do. This unfair disadvantage proves to be the unyielding force driving the growing gap between whites and minorities. Also, this is true in many white societies where blacks and other minorities find themselves around the world.

EDUCATION

In a society that is based more and more every day on one's credential, it is without question that the education gap between the haves vs. the have-nots is still present in our modern society. In spite of the universal education system that has been instituted in most of the modern nations, there remains a large inequality in the education that students receive which is largely based on economics. This is a systemic problem that every large metropolitan area in United States and countries around the world is facing: a large population of students, with what seems to be an ever-shrinking budget to provide adequate resources for those students. Unfortunately, a disproportionate number of working-class and working-poor minorities live in these metropolitan areas, which only go further to exacerbate the racial inequalities that already exist. Although several state Supreme Courts have ruled in recent years that the current method of funding public schools is unconstitutional, no major reforms have occurred in any of these states.

There is a significant trend of inequality in educational achievement across different races. According to the U.S. Department of Education, the social class, race, and ethnic achievement gap widened since 1998, despite continued educational policies aimed at reducing them. Asian Americans and whites have more success in education than African Americans and Hispanics. One possible explanation for racial inequality in education is that educational achievement is correlated with socio-economic status, and many inner-city school districts have high proportions of African American and Hispanic students.

Asian American students have the highest educational achievement in the United States. One study found that Asian Americans perceived themselves as more prepared, motivated and more likely to have higher career success than whites. The study also found that whites, African Americans, Native Americans, and Hispanics had the same perceptions of Asian Americans. One of the most consistent research findings on racial inequality is that black men receive considerably lower income returns on education than do white males. A breakthrough study of American men in the early 1960s concluded that black males generally begin in a lower starting position and enter a vicious cycle of being hindered at every step of the attainment process rather than move forward with ease. Their disadvantages are of the cumulative. They are less likely to obtain a higher education, and this is coupled with the fact that when they do, their occupational returns are less than those received by whites. Furthermore, the extended gap is also caused by the strong correlation between income inequality and mortality rates in African Americans.

The large inequality gap of blacks and whites could be directly related to education. In New York, some school districts are polar opposites when compared. The poverty-stricken regions of New York have public schools that are on average 90 per cent black and Hispanics and 10 per cent Asians, whites, and Middle Eastern. These underprivileged public schools have to content themselves with whatever personnel are left available, once the best trained have been hired by the more affluent schools. Physical installations and didactic equipment also tend to be lacking. These differences find repercussions as the children grow older: the underprivileged do not have opportunities to learn the social skills needed to perform adequately in socially higher milieus, and in addition to general below grade-level performances, this condemns them to subordinate, low-wage jobs. From this, a vicious cycle that equates to their children living the same lifestyle that they endured might ensue, along with a feeling of alienation.

Although there are prominent blacks like Colin Powell, Bill Cosby, Bryant Gumbel, Magic Johnson, Oprah Winfrey, Barack Obama, Michael Jordan, Michael Steele the present Republican chairman, and a host of others who are living comfortable lives, the whole black population is not as lucky. It appears that school integration peaked in 1967 and declined ever since. It is because of this odd system of inequality in education that President George W. Bush declared the No Child Left Behind Act during his administration. But still there is a lot to do in order to promote equality and integration in educational system in the US. Also, President Obama has called for improvement in the educational system so that they can produce graduates who can compete in a global economy. It is a shame that even after the Declaration of Independence of 1776 calling for equal rights and opportunities for all, America still dwells on and enjoys racism in every area of its society.

With what is still going on in the US educational system, the struggle by the civil rights movement to end all these has not really eliminated racism and inequality in America. It is not only celebrating the memory of Martin Luther King, but America and the rest of the world should also put to an end those things he fought against and died for. We also remember a lot of people whose names might be mentioned who fought and died in the cause of equal rights and opportunity for all. Remember President Kennedy's efforts to end racism in America, which actually led to conspiracy assassination of a noble man.

HEALTH

Life expectancy is a common measurement of one's health and is commonly used to gauge the quality of life in a group of people. A health study in 1999 looked at life expectancy for whites, blacks, Asian Americans, Native Americans, and Hispanics. For both men and women, Asian Americans were found to have the highest life expectancy at 59.13 more years for men aged 20, and 64.31 more years for women aged 20. Men among Native Americans and whites aged 20 had the next highest life expectancy to live 54.73 and 54.59 more years, respectively. They were followed by Latin Americans, who had a life expectancy of 48.97 more years after age 20. Finally, black men had the lowest life expectancy beyond 20 years of 47.58 more years.

Though life expectancy is a good indicator of quality of life, it does not usually separate active and inactive life expectancy. Living an active life plays a positive role in life expectancy, but the most important factor is receiving good and quality health care. In the United States and some Western European countries, people are assigned doctors based on their class, race, and ethnicity. The health sector is highly involved in institutional racism by their collective failure to provide appropriate and professional service to people irrespective of their race, colour, and ethnic origins. In the Netherlands for example, many immigrants of African descent have complained of the careless attitude of the Dutch health workers when it comes to treating blacks in health matters. Because of these feelings many Africans living in the Netherlands even prefer visiting Belgium for better medical treatment. The ethics of the profession of medicine has been neglected because of institutional racism in the health sector. I believe the life of a patient should override which colour of skin he or she has, because life is equal, no matter how unequal it might seem to those who practice racism.

CRIMINAL JUSTUCE SYSTEM

Racial inequality in the criminal justice system is a topic that has become increasingly more relevant with the rising penal population in the United States. Education and race seem to be the most decisive factors when deciding who goes to jail and what age cohort has the greatest percentage chance of incarceration. Race inequalities in the criminal justice system have a strong effect in many realms of society such as family life, and employment. Going to prison no longer affects just the individual who committed the crime, but instead, the family and community left behind gain a new burden by one individual's actions. The United States still has a large disparity between whites and blacks and now a growing Hispanic population. This racial disparity in the educational system, job sector, and neighbourhoods have all contributed to the booming prison population in the latter part of the twentieth century which has only continued to widen in the twenty-first century.

Max Weber, a prominent sociologist, said race and ethnicity do play an important role in contemporary sentencing decisions. Blacks and Hispanic offenders—particularly those who are young, male, or unemployed—are more likely than their white counterparts to be sentenced to prison; in some jurisdictions, they also receive longer sentences than do similar white offenders. Likewise, racial profiling exists when certain people are targeted for heightened law enforcement scrutiny based on their race. Researchers confirm that blacks are more likely to be stopped in traffic by the police, and black women are nine times more likely to be X-rayed or subjected to intrusive searches by customs officers in airports.

Recently in Italy, a case involving the death of a British student was hastily decided without proper and exhaustive investigation. The case involved two whites and one black man; the black man was quickly sentenced to thirty years imprisonment, while the two whites involved are still going on trial. It is rare in Europe to see people who committed murder receive a thirty-year jail sentence even if it is double murder. And in this case, you wonder why the justice system in Italy is still trying to convict two white people, if the black man has been convicted as the offender and his fellow accomplices are still loose, even when there is evidence that the American lady involved has been giving conflicting evidence both in the court and to the police. In fact, this is just one case that is recent in the twenty-first-century world filled with human rights lawyers and Amnesty International. You hear Amnesty always calling for equal justice, even for mass murderers in Guantanamo Bay in Cuba. However, black men and other minorities and the poor will continue to be the victims of the white oppressive system design based on race.

RACE INEQUALITY IN PRISON

Sometimes you also have to admit the problems with black males, who prefer gangs to getting education and living a decent life. The story is the same in the US, Britain, the Netherlands, Germany, Spain, to mention but a few. It is true that the justice system is racially unequal when it comes to whites and minorities, but minorities such as blacks should concentrate more on how to avoid criminal circle, and empower themselves through education. You know the last time in court O. J. Simpson was crying, but I was laughing because he allowed the white man's criminal justice system to get hold of him. After he was acquitted in the murder case of his ex-wife, many white people were bitter about that. Based on this, they have laid a trap for him and he finally gave the criminal justice another golden chance to deal with him. He is one of the dumbest black men I have ever known in my life, though he was intelligent per se.

LIKELIHOOD OF GOING TO PRISON

The likelihood of black males going to prison in their lifetime is 16 per cent compared to 2 per cent of white males and 9 per cent of Hispanic males. If there is no substantial gap in the likelihood of committing a crime between races, then this report proves beyond a reasonable doubt that there is racial inequality in the criminal justice system. Other social factors can be linked to the racial inequality in the criminal justice system, such as socio-economic status, the environment you grew up in, and the highest educational level a person achieves.

This is the disadvantage of living in an oppressive and racial system filled with inequality, and this always creates and leads to tension and conflict with increase in criminal activity. For law, it is always easy to punish but difficult to save people.

RACIAL INEQUALITY IN DEATH PENALTY

There is also a large disparity between races when it comes to sentencing convicts to death row. Looking just at the US federal death penalty data released by the Department of Justice between 1995 and 2000, 682 defendants were charged with death-eligible crimes. Out of those 682 defendants, 48 per cent of the defendants were blacks. Hispanics were 29 per cent of the cases and whites only 20 per cent of the cases. But from media reports, we always see cases of whites every time involved in murder cases, such as killing of their own families as well as colleagues at workplaces. With these reports, you wonder if these cases are also included in the 20 per cent of cases of whites with death penalty. This is a question that has to be answered by those in authority, because many homicide cases involve fewer of black folks.

RACIAL INEQUALITY IN BAIL SETTING

Studies have documented racial disparities in the amount of money required for bail. For example, a study of Wake County, North Carolina found that African Americans had bail set at 18 per cent higher than whites charged with similar crimes. That is to say, when a black or white commits a crime of the same magnitude, the bail charges for a black person are higher than that of a white person.

CONTRIBUTING FACTORS TO THE RISE IN THE PENAL POPULATION

The United States features a prison population that is more than quadruple the highest prison population in Western Europe. In the 1980s, US legislation issued a number of new drug laws with stiffer penalties that range from drug possession to drug trafficking. Many of those charged with drug crimes saw longer prison sentences and less judicial leniency when facing trial. The war on drugs has furthered the boom in prison population even though violent crime has continued to decrease steadily. A lot of urban areas in the United States have a majority black population, and in these areas, drugs are also prevalent. This means that a greater percentage of those in prison are going to be black because the law enforcement is already concentrated in the areas with high violent crime and drug crime. With this new drug legislation, the US government increased the use of incarceration for social control, which resulted in sharper disproportionate effects on African Americans. In politics, blacks are still in the minority when it comes to winning legislative seats in the state and federal government. Because of this, legislation is being formed and issued through the eyes of the white majority in Congress, which has led to the continued burden in black communities across the United States.

Blacks are presented as being in majority in crime cycle, but the fact is that the law enforcement are always going after petty criminals while the big fish in crimes are left out. Drug cartels and barons in the

United States and around the world are not blacks. A black can go to jail for possession of a milligram of drugs, but white celebrities will go free for possessing even half a kilogram. This shows also the nature of inequality in US criminal justice system. We have seen from news reports how white stars in Hollywood escape the long arm of the law when they are involved in crimes that deserve prison terms. The case of Polanski, the film director who has avoided sentencing since he was accused of rape, is recent in people's mind.

FACTORS CONTRIBUTING TO PEOPLE GOING TO PRISON

Blacks have a higher chance of going to prison especially if they drop out of high school. The importance of getting a high school education is the difference between going to prison and functioning as a good citizen in society. If a black male drops out of high school, he has a 32.4 per cent chance of going to prison while his white and Hispanic counterparts have a 6.7 per cent and 6 per cent chance respectively. Bruce Western and Becky Petit use the example of the age cohort that grew up during the Great Depression. These men had to learn to value economic security because of the mass unemployment during the 1930s. They delayed marriage and fatherhood in order to establish themselves with economic security to provide for the families and became the 'greatest generation' in America. In latter part of the twentieth century, the age cohorts born in this time period never experienced a major event in their lives like the less-educated individuals especially among minorities.

Less education in urban areas tends to lead to negative influences on children growing up in this situation. Children who have a parent in prison are easily influenced by older children in their neighbourhoods. They are then exposed to the life of drugs and violent crime that can lead them to join gangs and follow the same path as those adults in their neighbourhoods who are incarcerated.

EFFECTS ON FAMILIES AND NEIGHBOURHOODS

From the criminal justice system, we see how institutions of society have great power to reward and penalise. They reward by providing career opportunities for some people and foreclosing them for others. They reward as well by the way social goods and services are distributed, by deciding who receives training and skills, medical care, formal education, political influence, moral support and self-respect, productive employment, fair treatment by the law, decent housing, self-confidence, and the promise of a secure future for self and children.

RACISM, CIVIL RIGHTS, AND TENSION

The racist attitude of white America against the blacks created tension and conflict among the population of the United States. It also gave room for the civil rights struggle against oppression and demand for equal rights and opportunities for all in US history. African slaves were imported into America against their will and were used to build the United States, yet were refused equal opportunity or participation in a democratic society that they helped to establish. The civil rights movement in America was one of the greatest movements in history, with its non-violent ideology, though sometimes violence ensued or occurred when things got out of hand.

According to the Bolsheviks, everything must have an end—the patience of the nation has come to an end, and the ice of silence has to be broken so that the people's movement can begin to flow; so sometimes the patience of the civil rights movement was broken and some took violent action, but most of the struggle was a peaceful movement until the death of Martin Luther King. He was also a victim of racists' white supremacy as well as President John F. Kennedy, because he had the idea of promoting equality and eliminating racism in America.

The Birth of a Nation (1915) by D. W. Griffith is a film that proclaims the European/white racists' inequality in America. The hero of the film was a member of the Ku Klux Klan (KKK), a white supremacy organisation in the USA, built on the idea of the white-only or superior-race ideology that still plays a major role in today's America. In Shelbyville in the State of Kentucky in 1901, 320 blacks were lynched to death after the death of a white woman. So compare the unequal measure of the white civilised society. The law also was silent in this case when men took it upon themselves to apply law while the state apparatus to administer justice was silent and powerless.

After the end of American Civil War, when slavery was abolished in 1865, slaves were liberated and given citizens' rights and political rights. Until 1890, they made use of their civil rights, including election rights. Blacks were elected to both state and federal legislature. By the beginning of the twentieth century, the United States went into a racist phase in her history. In 1896, the Supreme Court ruled in favour of equality of all citizens. The white authorities in the South began a bloody resistance against equality. Jim Crow adopted a racial inequality attitude to resist the Supreme Court ruling in the South. He and his Southern partners hindered black Americans from registering for voting and exercising their voting rights. The Ku Klux Klan started lynching blacks without due process of the law. From 1900 to 1917, about 1,241 blacks were lynched to death, and the worst was that nobody was convicted for most of these crimes against the black people.

By the 1920s, the KKK used the highest racial violence against African Americans (blacks), also against Jews and Catholics. With its five million members in the South and West of the US, they perpetrated racial atrocities against their victims. However, during this period, the African American Booker T. Washington told his fellow blacks that the best way forward for the blacks in America is for each one to better his/her life despite the racism. The white respects you (black) if he/she sees your two-story building. Booker T. Washington's assertion is true, but also if you are limited by law from owning property and being able to acquire, you can overcome, with hard and determined work.

Racial profiling was used in the twentieth century to stop immigrants from entering the USA. United States was influenced by racist scientists who warned that America would be polluted by genes of Asians, Spanish, and South European Jewish immigrants. Japanese and Chinese were considered dangerous in the American society.

Because of the tension mounting in the South and racial inequality there, many blacks moved to the North and West such as in Harlem, New York, working in the areas of music and arts. The jazz music developed by the blacks became popular in the Western world. In nightclubs, some black artists were not allowed inside, though the North was better in terms of racism /unequal treatment meted out to the black Americans. Blacks organised themselves to fight and struggle against racism and inequality. W. E. Du Bois started in 1905 the Niagara movement, which later became known as the National Association for the Advancement of Colored People (NAACP) and its 100th year was celebrated on 17 June 2009. It was amazing that the first African American president, Barack Obama, could address this noble organisation on its 100th anniversary. This confirms what Bob Marley said: Stand up for your right and do not give up the fight. The NAACP was followed by Booker T. Washington, who by the 1960s struggled for political rights for blacks. They solicited for integration, equal rights, and opportunity irrespective of skin colour. However, Marcus Garvey, who was Jamaican born, started preaching for all black people in the United States to go back to Africa. The white society was also against his mission and opinion, saying that he wanted to take the good Negros out of America. Can you imagine that—they do not want to live together with you as equals but also do not want you to go back to your roots?

In 1939, a white group called the Daughters of the American Revolution refused to allow famous black singer Marian Anderson to perform in their concert building in Washington DC. She was selected to sing at the Lincoln Memorial for First Lady Eleanor Roosevelt as a protest against racism.

In December 1941, Japan attacked the USA at Pearl Harbour; three months later, President Roosevelt signed order 9066, in which more than 100,000 Japanese were rounded up and locked up in a camp, even though some were already US citizens. Though Italy and Germany were also at war with the USA, their immigrants in the United States were left untouched, maybe because they were whites and Japanese were considered not white but yellow. In 1932, Roosevelt became president and promised the American people a New Deal; many of his programs became racist in action and discriminated against blacks. However, many blacks made gains during his time in new job opportunities, housing, and education. Racism was reduced in government offices, cafeterias and in 1937, he appointed the first black federal judge.

During the Second World War, in 1941, the USA was also known for its racist and inequality attitude where most black soldiers were not allowed military jobs. Also, her attitude towards Japanese was as racial enemy; this led to the arrest of Japanese in 1942 and they ended up in prison camps even though some were American citizens. American war propagandists drew Japanese as a minor race and ridiculous caricature with tiny eyes, and as monkeys. However, Roosevelt also banned discrimination by putting blacks in the ministry of defence. Many blacks started to work in defence industries in Detroit, Los Angeles, and Chicago. Black US soldiers stationed in England were surprised by the absence of racism in England. A lieutenant in the army wrote to his father: The more I see the English, the more I feel disgusted with the USA. He said after the war, he would start a movement to take white Americans back to England and white English to the United States. This shows how terrible the whites' racism was and its effects on the black Americans in those days and even till today, when it has been modified and became a silent killer disease.

It was racism that gave rise to the Holocaust, which took place in Europe. The killing of six million Jews in Germany was a result of racist theory. Racist ideology made Hitler create Nazism and a slave empire where non-Aryan races were considered slaves to be deprived of education, because he said if slaves become educated, they enjoy it and can become developed. This also the United States did to people after fighting against this ideology of Hitler and his like. The Nazis introduced an experiment of building a pure Aryan race; children from Slavic families were taken away from their parents and were used as genetic material. They were placed in German families or taken to farmlands in order to use them to create Aryan pure race. Homosexuals and people with handicaps were killed because Nazis said that they were incomplete genetically. In 1941, Nazis decided to create a pure European race and said that all Jews in the whole of Europe should be arrested—children, women, and men—and killed. It was a genocide project, extermination of Jews. There were also over 25,000 black German people who were killed as well or castrated. Reinhard Heydrich gave his plan on how to eliminate all the Jews in Europe, especially places under the Nazis' control, and the people bought his idea since they were like him in their racist ideas.

CIVIL RIGHTS MOVEMENT IN THE UNITED STATES 1955–1968

The civil rights movement was born out of the results of inequality—unequal treatment meted against African Americans by their own country. Inequality creates tension, uneasiness in the minds of those who are victimised by it. And as a result, the people have the right to resist it and the final end point will be tension, crisis, and conflict if not addressed earlier, be it in the United States, Asia, Africa, Europe, or the Middle East. Gandhi of India said that he had the right to disobey or resist unjust laws, and out of this came the civil rights movement, and resistance against racism and inequality in the United States. Inequality has become the bane of all instability and tension around the globe. The simple biblical injunction (natural law of equality) is to treat others the same way you would like to be treated.

If we humans, individually and collectively, could abide by this principle, I believe (and you know too) that we might live in a world community with limited tension and peaceful climate for all to enjoy. The late Michael Jackson sang the song 'Heal the World': Make the world a better place for you and for me. If we can heal the world of the disease of inequality, we all together can make this world a better place. So let us abandon racism and unequal treatment against one another. Medgar Evers of Jackson, Mississippi, before he was brutally murdered by white racists in 1963, said, 'If I die, it will be for a good cause. I have been fighting for America just as much as soldiers in Vietnam.' He was assassinated in his quest for equality.

Brown v. Board of Education of Topeka in 1954 decided to promote equality in all aspects of American society, where the nation's segregated schools limited blacks' opportunity for education before 1954. You know, every battle has its public and private moments of defeat and victory. Every historical moment is made of a multitude of personal experiences. Even drinking water was segregated in the United States but the people's struggle conquered it. As they said, 'we shall overcome one day.'

MEDIA INEQUALITY

The media was also involved in practicing racism and inequality, though there are times racists will be unable to hide everything. Martin Luther King Jr. said that the media is a spotlight that exposes and thereby halts the secret actions, a light that imprisons the imprisoner, so he decided to make use of the media for his struggle for freedom. King knew that the camera was helping to dismantle the arsenals of the oppressors. The organisers of the Birmingham march of 1963 movement staged conflicts for the media to publicise. The images of police brutality and repression were published all around the world and America, and this attracted sympathy, financial support, and political backing for freedom for the movement.

This was the cold war period when United States of America projected an image of Americans guarding and encouraging democracy around the world. And he said that the Birmingham pictures made him sick. The *Washington Post* reported Harris Wofford wrote to President John F. Kennedy that ending discrimination in America would do more to promote good relations with African leaders than anything else. After the Birmingham incident, the president initiated a bill that was passed after his death, which would become the Civil Rights Act of 1964. This changed the status and position of blacks in America, though the inequality and racism persist till today on a lower scale. During the cold war and antifascism, white media in the USA were able to portray black struggles when they had in the past ignored positive images of African American life and suppressed portrayals of black political actions.

In 1938–9 in New Madrid County, Missouri, during winter, landowners sought to evict hundreds of blacks and white tenant farmers so that cheaper day labourers could be hired instead. Owen Whitefield, a black Baptist preacher, organised the Southern Tenant Farmers' Union. He persuaded the sharecroppers to mount a protest. The 1,300 displaced farmers pitched camps along a hundred-mile stretch of highways 60 and 61. The protest received extensive coverage in newspapers across the nation, but blacks were given scanty chances in the reports and photographs published, even though more than 90 per cent of the protesters were black. The role of the black organizers was omitted altogether. Photographs that gave a better indication of black activism were made by Arthur Rothstein (a farm security Administrative photographer, but was not published at the time. Emmet Till's lynching in 1955 received a different kind of coverage that was new in USA. Racial lynching—abduction and murder of black men by white mobs was the most extreme form of the physical intimidation that undergirded so much American racism prior to the civil rights movement.

In 1953, 43 per cent of Americans had television, but by three years later, 83 per cent of USA households had access to TV. The television and satellite helped the civil rights movement. The March to Washington in 1963 was the largest demonstration in the United States history till date, was one of the first events to broadcasted live all around the world. Martin Luther King won the Nobel Peace Prize in 1964 because of his struggle for equal rights and freedom for the oppressed blacks of America. The press presented the images of booted and helmeted state-employed thugs attacking civilians—iconography of fascism that shocked many viewers into sympathy for the oppressed, the images from Birmingham, Selma, and Alabama of 1965. On 7 March 1965, ABC broadcast the images of state troopers stampeding and beating peaceful marchers. 'The hideous parallel between Auschwitz and Selma was obvious even to the insensitive,' wrote Warren Hinckle and David Welsh of ABC news in *Ramparts*.

Student Nonviolent Coordinating Committee (SNCC) was instrumental to the civil rights movement as regards to communication, and photographs. The director James Foreman was a communication genius. John Lewis (now a congressman) was the former chairman, saw in an early issue a Congress of Racial Equality advertisement. The news media was effective and important for the safety and lives of the civil rights movement, said Mary King. James Foreman recognised the power of photographs because these bear witness as events unfold. They say power did not concede willingly, as it never does. The civil rights movement was American's second revolution and formed a model for social struggle around the world for justice.

Lynching, a home-grown form of American terrorism, used to scare off blacks from voting and seeking other rights. It had begun in the Reconstruction Era directly after the Civil War and was spread by the Ku Klux Klan. Walter Chivers, Martin Luther King Jr.'s sociology professor at Morehouse College estimated that in the South between 1880 and 1922, a lynching was perpetrated every two and a half days. The law and the press ignored these murders even though they were often carried out in public, with advance notice and with the cooperation of leading white citizens. Rosa Parks' and King Jr.'s anthem 'We Shall Overcome' used by the civil rights movement has since been used in Tiananmen Square (China, 1989), Leipzig, Johannesburg (South Africa), where the oppressed demanded freedom.

Emmet Till, a 14-year-old boy, was brutally murdered for flirting with a white girl (shopkeeper). The murderers were all acquitted; they later confessed the murder to writer William Bradford Huie for $4,000. The mutilation of Emmet Till was carried by both white and black publishers' press. Anne Moody recalled, 'Before Emmet Till's murder, I have known the fear of hunger, hell, and the Devil. But now there is a new fear known to me: the fear of being killed because I am black. This is the worst fear of my life . . . I did not know what one had to do or not to do as a Negro to be killed.' In 1955, Moody later became active in the Congress of Racial Equality (CORE).

The South of the USA was the most segregationist, where even newspapers such as *Negro News* were relegated. In the early 1960s, *Montgomery Advertiser* chief photographer Charles Moore confirmed this story. The black photographers/photojournalists made a lot of contributions to the civil rights movement, whether working for the black press or white press, since they had access or opportunity the white photographers did not have, and some of them were Gordon Parks, Frank Dandridge, and Joffrey Dark.

Racial inequality continues to tear the United States and its neighbourhoods apart. In many ways, things have gotten worse in the United States since the civil rights movement era. The story of America's inequality progresses shamelessly. In 1989, 1 per cent of the population owned 37 per cent of wealth; 86 per cent of the wealth was controlled by 10 per cent of the people. In 1992, 33.3 per cent of black Americans' incomes were below the poverty line, compared to 11.6 per cent of whites. African Americans continue to fare worse economically than any other racial group in the United States (*Invisible Man*—Ralph Ellison, 1992). Gordon Park (1940) believed the camera exposed the evil of racism, evils of poverty, discrimination, and bigotry, by the people who suffered most under it.

James Cameron, who is the founder of the Black Holocaust Museum in Milwaukee, narrowly escaped being hanged in 1930 in Indiana, to be precise, on 9 August 1930. At least if you look at his contribution today, then you can imagine what the Negros in America lost by action of racism and its associated ills. In fact, in 1954 Alan Paton said about the Negro in America, 'These people through their struggles to achieve their basic rights as citizens are re-educating us to the meaning of true Americanism.' Also in 1958, Arnold Toynbee said, 'It may be the Negro who will give the spiritual dynamic to Western civilization that it so desperately needs to survive. The Negro may be God's appeal to this age—an age drifting rapidly to its doom.'

In 1957, the Southern Christian Leaders Conference (SCLC) was born, with Martin Luther King Jr. as its president. This later became the greatest and most powerful civil rights organisation. In March 1957, King and Coretta, his wife, were invited to the Independence Day of Ghana, the first African nation south of the Sahara to become independent. King Jr. was impressed by 'the intense democracy of African Negro deriving from tribal life' and that Ghana's independence has been achieved by non-violent method. By 1960, seventeen African countries had become independent too. Segregated schools violated the 14th Amendment of the United States Constitution, ruled Supreme Court judge Oliver Brown in 1954. The southern United States had over 100 congressional representatives in 1956, and this group called the decision by the Supreme Court unconstitutional and pledged to reverse it, in places like Alabama and Mississippi. In 1961, the inauguration speech of President John F. Kennedy called for all Americans to struggle for freedom around the world. Ross Barnett, the then governor of Mississippi in 1962 physically barred a black student, James Meredith, from registering in high school, saying that there was no case in history where the Caucasian race survived social integration.

SIT-INS AND FREEDOM RIDES 1960–1962: 'THIS WAS THE ANSWER'

In February 1960, four black students refused to leave a lunch counter if not served. Nevertheless, the restaurant refused to serve them because they were black, but they sat in the place until closing time, without being arrested. This happened in Greensboro, North Carolina, and the manager told them, 'You are not served here.' The white is good and intelligent, but when obsessed with racial superiority, he becomes stupid and ignorant of the law to the highest degree.

By mid-April of 1960, 50,000–70,000 sit-ins in restaurants had taken place in all the Southern states in the United States, supported by white students as well. The four that started the protest of sit-ins were Franklin McCain, Ezell Blair Jr., Joseph McNeil, and David Richmond. Most of the sit-ins were tutored by Lawson, and many of their methods were Lawson's idea of Gandhi's no-violence method he learned in India. White thugs in connivance with the police attacked most of their demonstrations. Robert Moses, a 26-years mathematics teacher, gave the phrase 'This was the answer.'

Martin Luther King Jr. was arrested in Georgia two weeks before the election between John Kennedy and Richard Nixon. Kennedy helped release King from four months' imprisonment based on traffic violation. Black voters were crucial in Kennedy's close victory over Nixon.

In 1961, John Lewis (now congressman), one of the great members of the civil rights movement, said he tasted Chinese food for the first time in his life, mixed with fear. During the days of sit-ins, Robert Zellner, the first white field secretary of the civil rights movement, said, 'The tragedy here is the work of people who believe in an idea enough to kill for it.'

'The problem of Mississippi is the problem of the nation and the world. A way has to be found to change this desire to kill,' Bob Moses said about the Ku Klux Klan's destruction of churches and killing of blacks and white civil rights activists. In 1964, during the sit-ins and bus boycott, many quotes emerged, such as Mother Pollard, who said, 'My feets is tired but my soul is rested.'

'How long? Not long, cause the arc of moral universe is long but bends towards justice,' said King Jr. on Selma 1964.

As the Voting Rights Act passed on 6 August 1965, Foreman said, 'If we can't sit at the table of democracy, then we will knock the fucking legs off.' Pam Clemson, a 17-year-old white girl who joined the struggle against racism and called herself 'a 17-year-old and out to save the world', was arrested and jailed for days.

BLACK POWER AND THE MARCH AGAINST FEAR, 1966

THE OPPRESSED AGAINST THE OPPRESSOR, BY MALCOLM X

Malcolm X was not a directly a part of the civil rights movement of non-violence. He criticised Martin Luther King Jr. for non-violence, the idea that when slapped on one cheek, you turn the other cheek too. He told people that when slapped one time, they should slap back more times. His anger grew out of his personal experiences of racism and inequality perpetrated by the white man in America. He stood apart in fearless rejection of the white society by black people. His style was of militancy. He said to Coretta King, if the white knows what the alternative is, they might listen to Dr King more easily. He said that America has no moral conscience.

Through Malcolm X's preaching, some blacks became violent also during the movement days. Organisation like the Black Panthers took some extreme positions in the struggle against inequality and racism in America. There were occasions when they also killed some people or attacked them with bombs, though their violent actions were by no means anything compared with violence perpetrated against the blacks in America by the state apparatus of terror aided by the Ku Klux Klan terrorists. We all know Bob Marley said that to every action, there is a reaction, so the violent reaction that began to emerge during the civil rights days was a result of the hideous acts of violent crime committed against innocent blacks. They were attacked with dogs, beaten, lynched to death, and killed by terrorist bomb attacks even at churches. The effects of inequality breed tension, violence, and conflicts, so for the world and societies to overcome these crises, we have to address the cause of inequality and racism.

'IT IS NOT OVER', 1965–1968

Martin Luther King Jr. told reporters that Watts was 'a class revolt of the underprivileged against the privileged'. The black power movement created a backlash from the white majority. The Carmichael leadership infused with the black power slogan divided the civil rights movement and brought negative impact to the course of the Negros. Television aided the passage of the civil rights legislation but also permitted the rapid mobilisation of adverse white reactions to Negro violence in the wake of the Watts riots.

Chicago, the second largest city in the United States as of 1965, was the most segregated residential area in the US. King felt that the rights of African Americans and Vietnamese children were linked—that he could not speak up for one without speaking up for the other. He believed that campaigning for justice and peace must be a global moral obligation for all. The money spent on war and defence can far better been spent on the black poor and on all the poor of the United States. After this comment, the then FBI head J. Edgar Hoover accused King Jr. as an agent of the Soviets and communism and sought that King be stopped or taken care of. By 1967, Martin Luther King Jr. adopted the tactic of civil disobedience to dislocate the functioning of a city without destroying it. He said it could be more effective than a riot because it can be longer lasting, costly to the society, but not wantonly destructive. He said the solution to poverty is to abolish it directly. Civil disobedience is also difficult for government to quell by superior force.

By spring of 1967, Marian Wright (now Edelman), an attorney of the NAACP, took the Senate Committee on poverty to Mississippi to see first-hand the devastated condition of living there. Senator Robert Kennedy told Marian to tell Dr King to bring the poor people to Washington. When King heard of the idea, he accepted it as a revelation. After Martin Luther King's assassination in 1968, over 100 US cities witnessed riots which left forty-six people dead nationwide, all of whom were whites, but only five blacks. It was the most concentrated racial violence in United States history. It was exactly on 4 April 1968 at Memphis that Dr King was assassinated by James Earl Ray.

The only real revolutionary, said King, is a man who has nothing to lose. Millions of people in the United States and around the world have little or nothing to lose. If they were helped to take action together, they would do so with freedom and power. That will be the new unsettling force in our complacent nation life. With these ideas in the minds of the oppressed to create tension that might explode any day or any time as dynamite, it should not be ignored by the political authorities around the globe. Inequality is the by-product of tension, violence, and associated danger of terror.

'I DO NOT MIND BEING BITTEN BY A DOG'—BIRMINGHAM, 1963

In 1963, Birmingham (Alabama), the largest city still segregated as in South Africa's apartheid government, Bull Connor and whites in the South refused to comply with the federal government order to desegregate. Instead, they closed swimming pools, parks, and sports centres. At the time, this city was called Bombingham, because of its excessive and continued bombing attacks on black houses, churches, and businesses, with none of the terror attackers brought to justice.

MARCH ON WASHINGTON

'WE STOOD ON A HEIGHT'

In 1963, there was a march to Washington, and before this time, in 1941 Philip Randolph had organised one under President Franklin Roosevelt, demanding guarantee of jobs for black men and women in the wartime. Roosevelt issued the first executive order protecting African American rights since the emancipation from slavery. Randolph also succeeded in persuading President Harry Truman to ban racial discrimination. The Washington march included a wide range of issues: unemployment, freedom, civil rights, etc. It was planned by the big six civil rights organisations, with Randolph and Bayard Rustin heading it. They pressed for the civil rights bill that was waiting in Congress. This march was organised with the support of men of President Kennedy.

The Washington march was held at the Lincoln Memorial, where Obama's inauguration was held on 20 January 2009, exactly forty-five years after Martin Luther King's speech 'I Have a Dream': Where men will be judged based on the content of their character and not by the colour of their skin. It was a fulfilment of his dream. From Roosevelt, Lincoln, George Washington, LBJ, Truman, and Kennedy with a host of other white people who understood the dignity of man helped to bridge the gap created by white racists. The racists committed a lot of crime against blacks, which culminated in the darkest history of America and the entire world.

> *When I was growing up I was bitten by a dog for nothing, so I don't mind being bitten by a dog for standing up for freedom. —Martin Luther King Jr.*

On Sunday, 15 September 1963, a youth celebration day, a bomb planted by white racists exploded in a church at Birmingham, killing four black girls. Two months later, on 22 November 1963, President Kennedy was assassinated in Dallas by whites aggrieved that he freed blacks from inequality, racism, and hatred. On 24 July 1964, the civil rights bill was passed into law by Congress. We all remember President Kennedy and others who helped to tear down the walls of injustice, inequality, and racism.

Fannie Lou Hammer shared her experience before President Lyndon Johnson (known as LBJ); she said, 'I was evicted from my job and home because of my involvement in the voters registration campaign in Mississippi and I was tortured in jail. Is this America, the land of free and home of the brave, where we are threatened daily because we want to live as decent human beings?' This statement embarrassed the president, and I believe it made him contribute his own quota in making laws that reduced racism and inequality in America by giving black Americans the right to vote in August 1965.

However, inequality is a disease that afflicts all humankind, and it needs a vaccine to inhibit its spread before it becomes pandemic if it has not already. During the days of the civil rights movement, there was also an issue of gender inequality which existed in the hierarchy of the movement, as it continues to exist today in many republics. Actually, Mary King and Casey Hayden discovered this in the civil rights movement and protested against inequality in Student National Coordinating Committee (SNCC). They agitated against lack of equality in the hierarchy and functions of the organisation. The top occupied by black men, followed by white men, white women and finally black women at the bottom (1967). With this initiative, liberation of women campaign took off in April 1966. It is obvious that when we solve one problem of inequality, there is a probability that we create another, but it is in the interest of the world to have a just and equal society. This will make the world a better place, with less tension, rancour, hatred, and killings. For those who cry for peace, you had better be real and cry for equal rights and justice, because that creates ground for peace and harmony among all peoples. Heal the world and make it better place for you and for the entire human race and me.

RACIST STATE / APARTHEID SOUTH AFRICA

By the 1930s, one American mine engineer was in South Africa to work, but he was shocked over the way black African workers were treated. His wife cried until she got home, saying, 'The black people here are badly treated that they become afraid to look at white people.

'I think the black people are more decent than some white people,' she concluded. That seems true to me and may be to many others who are open-minded and without prejudice.

At the end of the nineteenth century, Britain portioned Africa and gave control of South Africa to the Netherlands immigrant farmers, the Boers. The defeat of the Africans in the war 1899–1902 brought the Zulus of Africa to the authority of the British Empire. In 1910, South Africa Union got self-rule under the British Empire and left in the hand of minority whites of the Boers of Dutch descent of the Zulu land. The black Africans majority were denied voting rights and were discriminated against. The 1913 Colour Bar law was enforced which banned African indigents from owning lands within a reserved area for the whites. Also in 1923, the racists' white government implemented another law that African blacks should have a special pass to be able to live in the cities.

In 1912, black Africans formed the African National Congress (ANC) as a pressure group to demand democratic changes and resist the racist, unequal laws. However, in the beginning, the ANC had not much influence over the white minority rule supported by their imperial brothers in Europe and the United States. The Asians and the mixed race in South Africa were not badly treated as the native South Africans, who are the rightful owners of the land; that was the act of inequality brought to African shores by the white man.

The Boers were richer than the English South Africans, and they controlled the government. Some of them were just poor farmers and worked in relatively paid salary. They were afraid of the black Africans that competed with them in the land and workforce or jobs. They supported and spearheaded the apartheid policy. During World War II, South Africa supported the Allied forces, but the Boers admired Hitler and his racists' policy. Even the sea beaches were divided into racial portions to suit the inequality attitude and racial policy.

In 1964, Nelson Mandela, who later became the first black president of South Africa, was condemned to life imprisonment for demanding equal treatment and rights for all South Africans. During his hearing, he said, 'In my struggle, I have fought for Africans against white-dominated rule and against black dominant rule. I want an ideal democracy, and free society where all men live in harmony together and have equal chance. This is the ideal I hope for in life and what I hope to achieve. If need be, this ideal I am ready to die for.' He was sentenced to life and spent twenty-seven years behind bars, only to be released in 1990, when President George Bush Sr. and De Klerk of South Africa ended apartheid regime.

By 1950, two years after the National Party of the Boers won election, they registered people according to race categories. Marriage between different races was banned. Every aspect of life in South Africa was separated based on racial differences. The Boers separated everything according to race: school, beach, hospitals, university, and banks only for white minority in another man's land. In 1974, the General Assembly of the United Nations consensus was reached to suspend South Africa from participation in international sports and cultural events because of her apartheid policy.

RESISTANCE AGAINST APARTHEID

The moment we introduce inequality in every sphere of life or society, there are bound to be tension, resistance, and conflict. It has been the by-product of inequality throughout the history of humankind. In the 1950s, the ANC organised a resistance campaign against the apartheid government through civil disobedience and protest march. Nevertheless, the apartheid regime was merciless in putting down the resistance. They arrested people without trial, used torture and assassination to put opinions, free speech, and protest down. By 1960, the ANC discovered that peaceful demonstration could no longer work; they resorted to armed struggle against the apartheid regime.

The ANC adopted the use of military tactics of sabotage with peaceful protest against the regime, but the success was limited. Anti-apartheid activists had to leave South Africa as a means to escape from the white authority in South Africa. Even in exile, some of them were followed by apartheid agents and were murdered. On 21 March 1960, South African police opened fire on black protesters against the regime policy. They killed 69 people and wounded 180 in the city of Sharpeville. Police were seen marching over dead bodies of people they killed as if they were dogs or pigs but not humans.

Also in the summer of 1976 in the city of Soweto, the part region of South Africa, police were used as an instrument of torture and assassination. However, in 1980, riots in the black regions and economic sanction on the apartheid regime were affecting her behaviour. Powerful multinational companies began to pull out of South Africa for fear of damage to their reputation.

In 1977, Steve Biko, the leader of black consciousness, was arrested with others. While he was awaiting trial in prison, he was beaten and tortured to death. The reality of his death was a well-kept secret by the regime until twenty years later when it was revealed after the end of apartheid, during the reconciliation process headed by Bishop Desmond Tutu. F. W. de Klerk, in 1990, accepted to end apartheid, lift the ban on the ANC, and release Nelson Mandela after twenty-seven years in prison with other political prisoners. Most laws of the apartheid policy were revoked and de Klerk chose full democracy. After this, it appeared that South Africa would break up in violent conflict due to anger in the whites.

The white government pushed Africans against themselves through the secret Inkatha Freedom Party of the Zulu, by supporting a violent conflict between them and ANC. White extremists threatened armed struggle to hold on to their supremacy and unequal ideology. However, Mandela used wisdom to convince the whites that South Africa should be a land of democracy, where all races should be together with equal opportunity. In 1994, a multiracial election was held, and ANC won under the leadership of Nelson Mandela. Later, a Commission of Reconciliation was instituted under Bishop Tutu to resolve the evils, ills of the apartheid regime. The blacks forgave the whites' apartheid regime the heinous crime of inequality and terror they perpetrated against them. What a people with a mind of forgiveness! However, since 1994, the ANC under majority black rule has assumed and has remained in power since then. South Africa has remained peaceful with all races living in harmony irrespective of the still existing racial divide and high crime rate, but there is hope for a better South Africa, where all men will live in peace.

The idea of superiority of one race, tribe, class, gender, and social status against others has been the cause of the ills of this inequality, be it in the United States, South Africa, Europe, Australia, India, China, etc. So we are being called to work towards a peaceful world where all men will be treated equally irrespective of the differences that might exist. Let us say no to political class, scientists, government, religion that exploits the concept of race and other forms of inequality; we should remember that we are all equal in death.

CHAPTER 3

Social Inequality

Social inequality refers to lack of social equality, where individuals in a society do not have equal social status. Instances that may be socially unequal include property rights, voting rights, freedom of speech and assembly, access to health care and education, as well as many other social commodities. Inequality socially created by matching two different kinds of process. The social roles in society are first matched to reward packages of unequal values and individual members of society are then allocated to the positions so defined and rewarded. Social inequality is different from economic inequality but they are linked. Economic inequality refers to disparities in the distribution of economic assets and income, while social inequality is caused by the unequal distribution of wealth.

Social inequality exists because of the lack of wealth in certain areas, and it prohibits these people from obtaining the same housing, health care, etc. as the wealthy in societies where access to these social goods depends on wealth. The degree of inequality in a given reward or asset depends of course on its dispersion or concentration across the individuals in the population. Social inequality is also linked directly to racial inequality and wealth in equality. The way people behave socially, whether it is discrimination, racism, etc., tends to trickle down on the opportunities and wealth individuals can generate for themselves.

A perfect example of this is in Thomas Shapiro's book *The Hidden Cost of Being African American*. Shapiro strives to demonstrate how unequal the playing field is for blacks and whites. For instance, middle-class families, one black and the other white, are given different opportunities in the housing market. The black family is denied a housing loan from a bank while the white family is approved, a noticeable incident, considering that home ownership is one of the main ways Americans acquire wealth. It is also a well-known fact that racism plays a part in most social problems the society encounters as it develops. The ability of people to compete in a given economic environment was determined by their social status in the society.

Bias theory blames the members of the majority, but sometimes the minority needs to bear the blame when minority tends to dominate the majority and creates conditions for social inequality to persist in the system to their benefit. In particular, bias theories blame individuals who are prejudiced or racist. Lyndon B. Johnson issued an executive order in 1967 called Affirmative Action, regarding employment with agencies in the federal government. The order said, 'The contractor will not discriminate against any employee or applicant because of race, colour, religion, sex, or national origin.

'The contractor will take affirmative action to ensure that employees are treated, during employment, without regard to their race, colour, religion, sex or national origin.'

This, if really applied, creates room for equal treatment based on ability, skill, and performance, thereby reducing racism and social inequality in the system. Farley added in his (2000:492) Notes that the fundamental argument for making special efforts to hire more minority workers or admit more minority students to colleges is that this practice is the only way to undo the harmful effects of the past and present discrimination and inequality.

HORIZONTAL SOCIAL INEQUALITY

This is inequality—economic, social, or others—that does not follow from a difference in an inherent quality such as intelligence, attractiveness, or skills for people or profitability for corporations. In sociology, this is particularly applicable to forced inequality between different subcultures living in the same society. In economics, horizontal inequality is seen when people of similar origins, intelligence, etc. still do not have equal success and have different status, income, and wealth.

Traditional economic theory predicts that horizontal inequality should not exist in a free market. However, horizontal inequality is observed in real and simulated 'free market' systems. To optimal economy the pare is one traditional approach to the problem. Even in simulated systems, inequality of identical actors arises to give 'the rich and poor'. Horizontal inequality affects an individual's well-being as well as his or her social stability and therefore needs to be addressed wherever it exists.

SOCIAL STRATIFICATION

In sociology and anthropology, social stratification is the hierarchical arrangement of the social classes, castes, and divisions within a society. These hierarchies are not present in state-level societies (as distinguished from hunting-gathering or other social arrangement). According to Peter Sanders, in modern Western societies, stratification depends on social and economic classes comprising three main layers: upper class, middle class, and lower class. Each class further is subdivided into smaller classes related to occupation. The term *stratification* derives from the geological concept of strata, or rock layers created by natural processes. Our society has become more stratified in the recent years than ever—the super-rich class and the poor-ridden class that has become victims of the stratified society.

We are going to see how the issue of stratification affects and creates social problems in our society such as in the caste cases.

CASTE

Castes are systems of occupation, endogamy, social culture, social class, and political power. Social group and cultural heritage determine the assignment of individuals to places in the social hierarchy. Although India is often now associated with the word *caste*, the Portuguese first used it to describe inherited class status in their European society. Discrimination based on caste is prevalent mainly in parts of Asia (Pakistan, India, Sri Lanka, Bangladesh, Nepal, and Japan) and Africa. UNICEF estimates that discrimination based on caste affects 250 million people worldwide.

English *caste* is from Latin *castus* 'pure', meaning 'cut off, segregated', the participle of *career* 'to cut off' (whence also *castration*). Application to Hindu social groups originated in the seventeenth century, via Portuguese *casta* 'breed, race, caste.'

CASTE IN EUROPE

Ancient Greek society divided into free people and slaves. Only free, landowning, native-born men could be citizens entitled to the full protection of the law in a Greek city-state (later, Pericles introduced exceptions to the native-born restriction). In most city-states, unlike Rome, social prominence did not allow special rights. In Athens, the population divided into four social classes based on wealth. People could change classes if they made more money. In Sparta, they gave all citizens the title of equal if they finished their education. Slaves had no power or status. Sparta had a special type of serf-like helots. Their masters treated them harshly and helots often resorted to rebellions. According to Herodotus (1X, 28–29), helots were seven times as numerous as Spartans. Every autumn according to Plutarch (Life of Lycurgus, 28, 3–7), the Spartan ephods would pro forma declare war on the helot population so that any Spartan citizen could kill a helot without fear of blood or guilt (cryptic).

Social class in Ancient Rome played a major role in the lives of Romans. Ancient Roman society was hierarchical. Freeborn Roman citizens were divided into several classes, both by ancestry and by property. The broadest division was by ancestry, between patricians, those who could trace their ancestry to the first Senate established by Romulus, and plebeians, all other citizens. Originally, all public offices were open only to patricians, and the classes could not intermarry. In addition, several classes of non-citizens with different legal rights were along with slaves, who had none.

MIDDLE AGES

According to an English cleric of the late tenth century, society was composed of the three orders: bellators (in Medieval Latin) or 'those who fight' (nobles and knights); oratores or 'those who pray' (priests and monks); and laboratores or 'those who work' (peasants and serfs). In Medieval Europe, the estates of the realm were a caste system. The population was divided into nobility, clergy, and the commoners. In some regions, the commoners divided into burghers, peasants or serfs, and the estate-less. Although originally based on occupation, one's estate was eventually inherited, because of low social mobility. Poland's nobility were more numerous than those of all other European countries were, forming some 8 per cent of the population in 1791, and almost 16 per cent among ethnic Poles. By contrast, the nobilities of other European countries, except for Spain and Hungary, amounted to a mere 1–3 per cent. In France, serfdom lasted legally until 1789. It persisted in Austria-Hungary until 1848 and abolished in Russia only in 1861.

CASTE IN AFRICA

Countries in Africa who have societies with caste system within their borders include Algeria, Burkina Faso, Cameroon, Chad, Ethiopia, Gambia, Ghana, Guinea, Guinea-Bissau, Ivory Coast, Liberia, Mali, Mauritania, Niger, Nigeria, Senegal, Sierra Leone, and Somalia.

The Osu caste system in Nigeria and Southern Cameroon derived from indigenous religious beliefs, discriminate against the Osus (people as owned by the deities) and outcasts. Similarly, the Mande societies in Gambia, Ghana, Guinea, Ivory Coast, Liberia, Senegal, and Sierra Leone have caste systems that divided society by occupation and ethnic ties. The

Mande caste system regards the Jonow slave caste as inferior. Similarly, the Wolof caste system in Senegal is divided into three main groups: the geer (freeborn/nobles), jaam (slaves and slaves' descendants), and the outcast neeno (people of caste). In various parts of West Africa, Fulani societies also have caste divisions. Other caste systems in Africa include the Borana caste system of northeast Kenya with the Watta as the lowest caste, the Tuareg caste system, and the Ubuhake castes in Rwanda and Burundi. Sahrawi Moorish society in Northwest Africa was traditionally (and still is, to some extent) stratified into several tribal castes, with the Hassane warrior tribes ruling and extracting tribute—horma—from the subservant Znaga tribes. Although lines were blurred by intermarriage and tribal re-affiliation, the Hassane considered descendants of the Arab Magil tribe Beni Hassan, and held power over Sanhada Berber-descended Zawiya (religious) and Znaga (servant) tribes. The so-called Haratin lower class, largely sedentary oasis-dwelling black people consider natural slaves in Sahrawi–Moorish society.

CASTE IN SPAIN AND PORTUGAL AMERICA

The Spanish and Portuguese colonists of the Americans instituted a relatively loose system of racial and social stratification and segregation based on a person's heritage. The system remained in place in most areas of Spanish America up to the time independence was achieved from Spain. Castes used to identify classes of people with specific racial or ethnic heritage. However, privileges or restrictions more related to race and wealth than to a clear, defined system of castes. Among the castes, racial classifications used then in Spanish America are peninsular, criollo, castizo, mestizo, cholo, mulatto, indio and Negro, maracucho.

CASTE IN CHINA

The Southern and Northern dynasties showed such a high level of polarisation between North and South that northerners and southerners referred to each other as barbarians. The Mongol Yuan Dynasty also made use of the concept; Yuan subjects were divided into four castes, with northern Han Chinese occupying the second lowest caste and southern Han Chinese occupying the lowest one.

Several dynasties of Northern and especially Southern China (the East Jin, Song Qi) had a social configuration divided mainly into two classes along political and cultural lines. The dominant noble class, Shizu (literally 'noble family'), controlled most of the government offices and functions in the court. Most of the time, they also had kingship ties to the emperor. The other class, Hanmen ('austere family'), was largely excluded from all aspects of political and cultural life.

Traditional Yi society in Yunnan was caste based. People split into the Black Yi (nobles, 5 per cent of the population), White Yi (commoners), Ajia (33 per cent of the Yi population), and the Xiaxi (10 per cent). Ajia and Xiaxi were slave castes. The White Yi were not slaves but had no freedom of movement. The Black Yi was famous for their slave raids on Han Chinese communities. After 1959, some 700,000 slaves were freed.

CASTE IN HAWAII

Ancient Hawaii was a caste society. People were born into specific social classes; social mobility was known but it was extremely rare. The main classes were

> Ali'I, the royal Suuwop class: This class consisted of the high and lesser chiefs of the realms. They governed with divine powers called mana.

> Kahuna, the priestly and professional class: Priests conducted religious ceremonies, at the heiau and elsewhere. Professionals included master carpenters and boatbuilders, chanters, dancers, genealogists, and physicians and healers.

Maka'ainana, the commoner class: Commoners farmed, fished, and exercised the simpler crafts. They laboured not only for themselves and their families, but to support the chiefs and kahuma.

Kauwa, the outcast or slave class: They are believed to be war captives, or the descendants of war captives. Marriage between higher castes and the Kauwa was strictly forbidden.

CASTE IN INDIA

The caste system in India is one of the worst and well-known castes in the world; some caste systems have outlived their usefulness. Indian society has been divided since ancient times into several thousands of groups, castes, or communities called jati. The phrase 'Hindu caste system' mixes up two different schemes—the Varna (class/group) theoretical scheme based on idealised Brahminical traditions and some medieval codes, and the jati system prevalent in Indian society since historical times, despite the present-day use of the same phrase to describe both varna and jati, some observers have claimed

> The Varna system is of no significance to an understanding of the present-day caste situation except in broad ideological terms. Any attempt to examine the caste system by fitting it into the classical Varna model would be of limited relevance in understanding its role in the socio-political processes of contemporary India.

VARNA

Early Indian texts like the Rigveda (10.90.12), Manu-smriti, and the Puranas speak of Varna, which means order, category type, colour (of things) and groups the human society into four types as follows:

1. Brahmins (scholars, teachers, priests)
2. Kshatriyas (warriors, kings, soldiers)
3. Vaishyas (merchants, agriculturists)
4. Shudras (workers, artisans, service providers)
5. Pariahs, or untouchables, are the bottom of social scale and perform the jobs nobody else wants such as raw sewage handling and killing animals; they live in special areas and are not allowed to read holy books.

I will not go into a bigger picture of the Indian caste system, because it is so complex that it needs to be taken care of in another book dealing specially on the castes in India. However all the Varnas were urged, without exceptions, to inculcate non-possessiveness, non-stealing, truthfulness, non-violence, and benevolence. These too were the very attributes propounded by the Jain and Buddhist doctrines. All others who did not subscribe to the norms of this Hindu society, including foreigners, tribals, and nomads, or even those who had been excommunicated, were called Mlechhas or Anaryas and were to be treated as contagious and untouchable. The fear of banishment from the society was seen as a major incentive not to violate its norms by its members. A late section of the most Shanti Parva of the Mahabharata suggests an origin of this practice: 'He who becomes harsh in speech, or violent in temper, he who seduces or abducts other people's women or robs the wealth that belongs to others, should be cast off by us.'

Many political parties in India have openly indulged in caste-based politics. Parties such as Bahujan Samaj Party (BSP) rely on the Dalits; the Rashtriya Janata Dal, the Samajwadi Party, and the Janata Dal rely primarily on the support of other backward castes and Muslims to win election. A UN report has slammed India for caste discrimination, which is a recognisable fact in Indian society; no matter how India tries to deny that, it is true and she should abolish it for good.

The issue about India caste is that it has been a big social problem and has been used to stratify the society in a way that it is racial and discriminatory. It has been used to humiliate and limit people from participating fully in a democratic setting. In addition, it runs contrary to UN's declaration against all forms of racism and discrimination. The international community needs to put pressure on India to bring this social problem to a stop because it contravenes all human principles.

CASTE IN KOREA

The baekjeong were an 'untouchable' outcast group of Korea, often compared with the burakumin of Japan and the Dalits of India and Nepal. The term baekjeong itself means 'butcher', but later changed into 'common' citizens to change the caste system so that the system would be without untouchables. In the early part of the Goryeo period (918–1392), the outcast groups were largely settled in fixed communities. However, the Mongol invasion left Korea in disarray and anomie, and these groups began to become nomadic. Other subgroups of the baekjeong are the chaein and the hwachae. During the Joseon dynasty, they were of specific professions like basket weaving and performing executions. They were also considered in moral violation of Buddhist principles which lead Koreans to see work involving meat as polluting and sinful, even if they saw the consumption as acceptable.

The opening of Korea to foreign Christian missionary activity in the late nineteenth century saw some improvement in the status of the baekjeong; however, not everyone was equal under the Christian congregation, and protests erupted when missionaries attempted to integrate them into worship services, the non-baekjeong finding such an attempt insensitive to traditional notions of hierarchical advantage. Around the same time, the baekjeong began to resist open social discrimination that existed against them. They focused on social injustices affecting the baekjeong, hoping to create an egalitarian Korean society. Their efforts included attacking social discrimination by the upper class, authorities, and 'commoners' and the use of degrading language against children in public schools.

With the unification of the three kingdoms in the seventh century and the foundation of the Goryeo dynasty in the Middle Ages, Koreans systemised their own caste system. At the top were the two official classes, the yangban. Yangban means 'two classes'. It was composed of scholars (munban) and warriors (muban). Within the yangban class, scholars (munban) enjoyed a significant social advantage over the warrior (muban) class until the Muban Rebellion in 1170. Muban ruled Korea under successive warrior leaders until the Mongol Conquest in 1253. Sambyeolcho, the private army of the ruling Choe dynasty, carried on the struggle against the Mongols until 1273, when they were finally wiped out to the last man in Chejudo. With the destruction of the warrior class, the Munban gained ascendancy. In 1392, with the foundation of Joseon dynasty, the full ascendancy of munban over muban was final. With the establishment of Confucianism as the state philosophy of Joseon, the muban would never again gain its former social standing in Korea society.

Beneath the yangban class were the jung-in. They were the technicians. They served in lower level government bureaucracy. They were literate, yet were unable to rise into full bureaucratic positions despite passing the gwangeo (central government entrance exam). This class was small and specialised. Beneath the jung-in were the chunmin. They were the landless peasants. These people composed majority of Korean society until the 1600s. They were illiterate, and forbidden from marrying into the yangban class. During the Japanese invasion of 1592, as many government genealogical records were burnt, many of them fabricated their social origin and moved to the yangban class. With the Manchu invasion of Korea in 1627 and 1637 and numerous peasant rebellions that followed, the ranks of yangban families swelled up to more than 60 per cent of the whole country by the late 1800s.

There was also the servant class called the sangmin. Underneath them all were the baekjeong, meaning 'butcher'. They originated from the Khitan invasion of Korea in the 1000s. After their defeat, the Goryeo government retained them as warriors, spread out throughout Korea. As they were nomads skilled in hunting and tanning of leather, their skills were initially valued by Koreans. Over centuries, their foreign origins were forgotten, and they were only remembered as butchers and tanners. Korea had also a very large slave population, nobi, ranging from a third to half of the entire population for most of the millennium between the Silla period and the Joseon dynasty. Slavery was legally abolished in Korea in 1894 but remained extant in reality until 1930.

With the Gabo reform of 1896, the caste system of Korea was officially abolished. However, the yangban families carried on traditional education and formal mannerism into the twentieth century. With the democratisation of the 1990s in South Korea, remnants of such mannerism and classism is now heavily frowned upon in the South Korean society, replaced by a belief in egalitarianism; however, in North Korea, there is still caste system in place.

CASTE IN NEPAL

The Nepal caste system resembles that of the Indian jati system, with numerous jati divisions with a varna superimposed.

CASTE IN PAKISTAN

A caste system similar to that in India is practiced in Pakistan. In the absence of 'classical' caste, typically the proxies used are ethnic background (Sindhi, Punjabi, Pusthun, Balochi, Mohajir, etc.), tribal affiliations, and religious denominations or sects (Sunni, Shia, Ahmadiya, Ismaili, Christian, Hindu etc.). While caste / social stratification information can be found relating to specific areas in Pakistan, it is not known if any studies have compared how relatively prevalent such attitudes are amongst the various ethnic groups, religious sects, and geographies. In addition, it is not known if any tracking studies have documented changes in these social attitudes.

Anecdotal evidence seems to suggest that there are quite significant differences in how the social stratification is practiced within and between the various ethnic and religious groups in Pakistan. The social stratification among Muslims in the Swat area of Northern Pakistan has been meaningfully compared to the caste system in India. The society is rigidly divided into subgroups where each quom (meaning 'tribe' or 'nation') is assigned a profession. Different quoms are not permitted to intermarry or live in the same community. These tribes practice a ritual-based system of social stratification. The quoms who deal with human emissions are ranked the lowest.

This system in Pakistan creates sectarian divide and strong issues. Lower castes (or classes) are often severely persecuted by the upper castes (or classes). Lower castes are denied privileges in many communities, and violence is committed against them. A particular infamous example of such incidents is that of Mukhtaran Mai in Pakistan, a low-caste woman who was gang raped by upper-caste men. In addition, educated Pakistani women from the lower castes may be at risk to be persecuted by the higher castes for attempting to break the shackles of the local, restrictive system that traditionally denied education to the lower castes, particularly women.

A recent example of this is the case of Ghazala Shaheen, a low-caste Muslim woman in Pakistan who, in addition to getting a higher education, had an uncle who eloped with a woman of a high-caste family. She was accosted and gang-raped by the upper-class family. The chances of any legal action are low due to the Pakistani government's inability to repeal the Hudood ordinance against women in Pakistan, though Pakistani president Prevez Musharraf proposed laws against Hudood, making rape a punishable offense, which were ratified by the Pakistani Senate. The law is meeting considerable opposition from the Islamist parties in Pakistan, who insist that amending the laws to make them more civilised towards women is against the mandate of Islamic religious law. Despite these difficulties, the law was passed and is now expected to help the situation in regards to women.

The late Nawab Akbar Bugti, the leader of his tribe fighting for the Balochistan Liberation Army, criticised Punjabi attitudes to women when he said, 'What respect we give to a woman, irrespective of her caste, religion or ethnicity, no Punjabi can understand.'

CASTE IN YEMEN

In Yemen, a caste-like system keeps the Al-Akhdam as perennial manual workers for the society, through practices that mirror untouchables. Al-Akhdam, literally meaning 'servant', is the lowest rung in Yemeni caste system and by far the poorest. According to official estimates, the total number of Khadem countrywide is in the neighbourhood of 500,000, of which some 100,0000 live in the outskirts of the capital Sana'a, while according to a *New York Times* article on 27 February 2008, there are more than a million. The remainder are dispersed mainly in and around the cities of Aden, Taiz, Labj, Abyan, Hodeidah, and Mukalla.

CASTE IN JAPAN

The two main castes in Japan are samurai warrior castes and peasants. Only the samurai was allowed to bear arms. A samurai had a right to kill any peasant whom he felt was disrespectful. Japan historically subscribed to a feudal caste system. While modern law has officially abolished the caste hierarchy, there are reports of discrimination against the Buraku or Burakumin under-castes, historically referred to by the insulting term Eta. Studies comparing the caste system in India and Japan have been performed, with similar discriminations against the Burakumin as the Dalits. The minority groups in Japan, along with the Ainu of Hokkaido, residents of Korea, and Chinese Burakumin are regarded as ostracised. The Burakumin are among the descendants.

It is shameful that modern society, with all its achievement in technology and democratic principles, should continue to allow this type of social problem with its ugliness to persist in our society. This should be the next line of revolution the international community needs to embark on to bring these ills to their knees.

ORIGIN

The Khadem are not members of the three castes—Bedouin (nomads), Fellahin (villagers), and Hadarrin (townspeople)—that comprise mainstream Arab society. They are believed to be of Ethiopian ancestry. Some sociologists theorise that the Khadem are descendants of Ethiopian soldiers who had occupied Yemen in the fifth century but were driven out in the sixth century. According to this theory, the al-Akhdam descended from the soldiers who stayed behind and were forced into menial labour as a punitive measure.

DISCRIMINATION

The Khadem live in small shanty towns and are marginalised and shunned by mainstream society in Yemen. Khadem slums exist mostly in big cities, including the capital, Sana'a.

Their segregated communities have poor housing conditions. Because of their low position in society, only a few children in the Khadem community are enrolled in school and often have little choice but to beg for money and intoxicate them with crushed glass. A traditional saying in the region goes, 'Clean your plate if it is touched by a dog, but break it if it's touched by a Khadem.' Though conditions have improved somewhat over the past few years, the Khadem are still stereotyped by mainstream Yemeni society, considering them lowly, dirty, ill-mannered, and immoral.

Many NGOs and charitable organisations from other countries such as CARE International are working towards their emancipation, while the Yemenese government denies that there is any discrimination.

By the general attitudes of Arabs and associated Muslims' beliefs, their attitude of discrimination and humiliation against non-Arabs and non-Muslims strictly contravenes humanity. Based on this, I believe strongly that they have no moral justification to criticise Israel on their same type of attitude against the Palestinians, though Israel's attitudes towards them are not justified too. Everybody wants to be free, and therefore the Palestinians should be allowed to live and enjoy independence and freedom. The Arabs are one of most racist people in the world, and they are also crying wolf for being hated and discriminated against; they should better search their hearts and begin to alleviate the chains of oppression they mete out against others. When you look at what they are doing in Sudan, Mauritania, as well as in Northern Nigeria and the rest of the Arab and Islamic countries, you will conclude that there is strong evidence to the facts.

NON-STRATIFIED SOCIETIES

Anthropologists tell us that social stratification is not the standard among all societies. John Gowdy writes of 'assumptions about human behaviour that members of market societies believe to be universal, that humans are naturally competitive and acquisitive, and that social stratification is not natural, do not apply to many hunter-gathering peoples'. Non-stratified egalitarian or acephalous (headless) societies exist which have little or no concept of social hierarchy, political or economic status, class, or even permanent leadership.

KINGSHIP ORIENTATION

Anthropologists identify egalitarian cultures as kingship-oriented because they value social harmony more than wealth or status. These are contrasted with economically oriented cultures (including states), in which status and material wealth are prized, and stratification, competition, and conflict are common. Kingship-oriented cultures actively work to prevent social hierarchies from developing, which could lead to conflict and instability. They do this typically through a process of reciprocal altruism. A good example is given by Richard Borshay Lee's account of the I King San, who practice 'insulting the meat'. Whenever a hunter makes a kill, he is ceaselessly teased and ridiculed (in a friendly joking fashion) to prevent him from becoming too proud or egoistical.

The meat itself is then distributed evenly among the entire social group, rather than kept by the hunter. The level of teasing is proportional to the size of the kill—Lee found this out the hard way, when he purchased an entire cow as a gift for the group he was living with and was teased for weeks afterwards about it (since obtaining that much meat could be interpreted as showing off). Another example is the indigenous Australians of Groote Eylandt and Bickerton Island, off the coast of Arnhem Land, who have arranged their entire society, spirituality, and economy around a kind of gift economy called renunciation. According to David H. Turner, in this arrangement, every person is expected to give everything of any resource they have to any other who needs or lacks it at the time. This has the benefit of largely eliminating social problems like theft and relative poverty. However, misunderstanding obviously arises when attempting to reconcile Aboriginal renunciation economics with the competition/scarcity-oriented economics introduced to Australian by Anglo-Saxon, European colonists.

This is also what happened in the Bible in the Acts of the Apostles 2:43–47, Life among the Believers.

> Many miracles and wonders were being done through the apostles, and everyone was filled with awe. All the believers continued together in close fellowship and shared their belongings with one another. They would sell their property and possessions, and distribute the money among all, according to what each one needed. Day after day, they met as a group in the Temple, and they had their meals together in their homes, eating with glad and humble hearts, praising God, and enjoying the goodwill of all the people. Moreover, every day the Lord added to their group those who were being saved.

At least, around two thousand years ago people knew how to share and live in egalitarian society, but today when we say we are more civilised and rich, we create unequal society that is breeding crime, tension, and conflict.

The economic crisis created by the greedy people in the banking sector is about to degenerate into creating a global conflict that many might imagine. The next revolution will be the poor of the world against the greedy rich goats. They forgot that greediness is a form of idolatry (Colossians 3:3, James 5:1–6, 1 Timothy 6:17–18). Today both the people in the world and the Christians alike have become equal yoke in the crime of greed. They will do anything to get rich, so they create imbalance in the society. Even Karl Marx hated the capitalist attitudes that support and increase inequality. Wall Street and other financial institutions around Europe created the worst depression or economic downturn since the Great Depression because of their greed. In fact, there is going to be a revolution of the poor against the super-rich in the global society soon.

STRATIFICATION

Class: A person's economic position in a society. Weber differs from Marx in that he does not see this as a supreme factor in stratification. Weber noticed how managers of corporations or industries control firms they do not own; Marx would have placed such a person in the proletariat.

Status: A person's prestige, social honour, or popularity in a society. Weber saw how political power was not just welded from capital value, but also their status, such as how poets or saints can have immense influence on society, but have relatively little economic worth.

Power: A person's ability to get his way despite the resistance of others. For example, individuals in state jobs, such as employees of the Federal Bureau of Investigation (FBI) USA, or a member of the United States Congress, may hold little property or status, but still hold immense power.

SOCIAL STRATIFICATION AND INEQUALITY

A staggering number of Americans currently live below poverty lines or levels. About 66 per cent of the poor are whites, reflecting the fact that whites outnumber people of other races and ethnic groups in United States. About 25 per cent of the people living in poverty are blacks. In 2005, about 16 per cent of children under age 18 years live in poverty, about 80 per cent of them live in households headed by single females. This is because of the problem emanating from divorce and broken homes in the United States of America.

It is so appalling that the richest country in the world has such levels of poverty, even among children, in a land where people spent 42 billion dollars last year alone on pets—dogs, cats, birds, etc. People have much money to spend on animals than on human beings irrespective of their much-acclaimed religious belief. The philosophy of materialism and capitalism has affected this nation more and even the rest of the world like a virus. Actually today's world has become more obsessed with materialism than any other time in human history. However, many will deny it. The way the gypsies of Europe are being treated proves what we are talking about. Many minorities living in Europe do not go far in terms of developing themselves because of the racial limitations posed before them in the society where they found themselves. Today many refugees living in Europe are not allowed to go to school beyond learning the language of the host country. Moreover, after learning the language, you cannot go further if you do not have a resident permit; you cannot work or learn a skill so long as you have no resident permit. And one funny thing about it all is even after studying the language you can be deported any time for not having a resident permit, and this occurs often when black African migrants are involved.

Recently we saw how Berlusconi, the Italian prime minister, in collaboration with the Arab racist Gaddafi, was deporting African migrants from Italy to Libya. That Berlusconi did not only dismantle homes of Roma or gypsies but also expelled many to Romania and Bulgaria. Recently, Sarkozy of France has followed suit in expulsion of Roma from France. He accused them of being responsible for crime waves in France. The unfortunate thing about this action is that a son of Jewish immigrants did this, the Jews rounded up in Europe and expelled from Germany and other places during the Nazi era. What a tragedy that Sarkozy is accusing the Roma the same way Europe, including France, accused the Jews around 1492 to the early 1930s. World population lives in abject poverty. This is the significance of a poll conducted across Europe, Asia, and the United States by the *Financial Times* of London and the Harris polling firm between May and June 2009.

INTERNATIONAL STRATIFICATION SYSTEM

According to 1979 report by the World Bank, because of industrial development (particularly in China, Indonesia, South Korea, and Singapore), poverty in East Asian nations has declined by more than half over the past decades. Nevertheless, 21 per cent of the population remained in poverty in 1995 with evidence of widening gaps between the rich and the poor. And that is the good news. In 1999, according to the Economic Policy Institute, the richest 10 per cent of the world population's income is roughly 117 times higher than the poorest 10 per cent, up from 79 times higher in 1980. Take China out of the equations and 1998 ratio.

Share of Global Income Going to the Richest 20% and Poorest 20% of the World's Population

Year	Share of Richest 20%	Share of Poorest 20%	Ratio of Richest and Poorest
1960	70.3%	2.3%	30 to1
1970	73.9%	2.3%	32 to 1
1980	76.9%	1.7%	45 to 1
1989	87.3%	1.4%	59 to 1

United Nations Human Development Report, 1992

In 2004, according to World Watch Institute's 'The State of Consumption Today;, 12 per cent of the world's population that lives in North America and Western Europe accounts for 60 per cent of the private consumption spending, while the one third living in South Asia and sub-Saharan Africa accounts for only 3.2 per cent.

Anna Tibaijuka, Habitat executive director, warned in 2004 before the release of 'The State of the World's Cities', 'how extremism is likely to flourish in the world's rapidly spreading slums if governments do not tackle the poverty that fuels it'. In 2030, an estimated five billion people will be urban dwellers, two billion of whom slum dwellers. Mere looking at the present situation in the world coupled with economic, political climate, more than that estimate are already living in slums.

The 2009 report says the global distribution of capabilities is extraordinarily unequal, and that this is a major driver for movement of people. Migration can expand their choices—in terms of incomes, accessing services, and participation.

CLASS AND ECONOMIC BASED OF CONFLICT

All kinds of economic organisations generate conflict between classes defined by common economic position.

1. People whose economic position or class is the same tend to act together as a group (Class Forsich).
2. Economic classes are the most important groups in society; their history is human history.
3. Classes are mutually antagonistic; the interests of different classes do not coincide in any way. Conflicts are inevitable and define how society develops.

It is obvious that we cannot completely eliminate social class differences but we can do something to reduce the gap between classes. The three classes, upper, middle, and lower classes can co-exist happily without conflict if we can manage the gap that exists so that one is not dominant over the other. We know that social class is sociologists' major predictor of beliefs, behaviour, lifestyle, and life itself. When the *Titanic* sank in 1912, 60 per cent of the first class survived, 40 per cent of the second class survived, and only 25 per cent of the third class did. It is well known fact that the middle class is a precondition of sustainable society. Nikolai Tilkidjiev observes the best political community is formed by citizens of the middle class, and that those states are likely to be well administered in which the middle class is large and stronger than either singly, for the addition of the middle class turns the scale and prevents either of the extremes from becoming dominant. For a number of social scientists, its shrinkage in recent decades in the United States and other countries is a cause of concern. Fortunately, a sizable percentage of the population considers itself middle class: 45.6 per cent according to 2002 NORC general social survey USA, including more than one quarter of high school dropped age 26–41.

Anatole France said something about the lower class: 'The law, in its majestic impartiality, forbids the rich as well as the poor, to sleep under the bridges, to beg in the streets and steal bread.' Today in countries like the United States as rich as she is, people are homeless in high majority, steal and beg. When you come to cities like Lagos, Nigeria, thousands of people sleep under the bridges and beg in the streets while the criminals and greedy rich people drive around in tinted-glass expensive cars. A country that is the sixth largest producer of oil in the world cannot provide common and simple social services for her citizenry.

Presently in the United Nations Human Development report, Nigeria ranked 156 in the less human developed countries in the world. In terms of middle class, I think it does not exist in that country. Most countries in Africa cannot talk of middle class; you only have the upper class and the poorest people living in the society. With the look of things, there is no way you can say there is middle class. Moreover, this is the contributing factor to the lack of developing capabilities in the states in the continent of Africa. I hope the anger in the minds of the population will one day boil over so that people can take arms against the political elites, possibly a replay of what former President J.

J. Rawlings did in Ghana, which has shaped that country today, putting it in a new part of democracy.

The philosophy of capitalism and materialism has the worst type of inequality in the recent years, to the extent one wonders what should provide the safety nets for those unable to compete because of problems such as age or physical or mental disabilities, or being limited by other social factors. There is need for the society to change its greedy attitudes and try to reduce the gaps between the haves and have-nots.

CHAPTER 4

Wealth and Income Inequality

According to Edward Wolff, wealth is the stuff that people own. The main items are your home, other real estate, any small business you own, liquid assets like savings account, credit deposit savings (CDS), and money market funds, bonds, other securities, stocks, and the cash surrender value of any life insurance you have. Those are the total assets someone owns. From that, you subtract debts; the main debt is mortgage debt on your home. Other kinds of debt include consumer loans, auto debt, and the like. The difference referred to as net worth, or just wealth.

Economists define wealth in terms of marketable assets, such as real estate, stocks, and bonds, leaving aside consumer durables like cars and household items because they are not as readily converted to cash and are more valuable to their owners for use purposes, while income refers to a flow of resources over time and represents the value of labour in the contemporary labour market and the value of social assistance and pensions. It is a valuable gauge of economic inequality.

Income is therefore what the average family in any given society uses to reproduce daily existence in the form of shelter, food, clothing, and other necessities. In contrast, wealth can be said to be a storehouse of resources, it's what families own and use to reproduce income.

According to the Wealth of the Nation report published October 2008, average income in Britain has risen under the Labour government—but the distribution of wealth remains a story of increasing inequalities, particularly evident on regional basis. The report, based on four million households' nationwide, was first conducted in summer 1996. The second study, from data collected in 1999, indicated how people have fared under New Labour government. The answer is unsurprisingly not that well. Nationally, there has been an average income of 9.6 per cent to 21,365 pounds. However, some areas in the South and parts of London have seen substantial rises in earnings while others have seen very low growth rates. The Outer Hebrides has even seen a fall in income. The figures do not take into account inflation.

Unsurprisingly, the highest average household incomes are greater in London and South East. These are the only regions where average household income is ahead of the national average (and income in these regions is 40 per cent higher than the North of England). The wealthiest people in the country are concentrated in London, with those in Central London, Blackfriars, Barbican, and Belgravia with average household income of over 50,000 pounds skewing average income London-wide.

Alan Greenspan, former chairman of the Federal Reserve Bank, made the case for wealth: 'Ultimately, we are interested in the question of relative standards of living and economic well-being. We need to examine trends in the distribution of wealth, which more fundamentally than earnings or income, represents a measure of the ability of households.' Those who argue for greater importance of income make the case that for wealth to have actually a significant impact on one's standard of living, it has to be translated into higher income.

In this chapter, we will dwell more on income and wealth inequalities in the USA, as the world's biggest world economy and model of democracy. However, we also look at other areas around the world to explain the concept of inequality in this area. I remember, in January 2007, the then US president Bush stated education's role in 'income inequality is real, it's been rising for more than 25 years.' He said the reason is clear; we have an economy that increasingly rewards education.

WEALTH AND INCOME INEQUALITY IN THE UNITED STATES

The last thirty years have seen a tremendous rise in income and wealth disparity in the United States and around the world. An issue of *Multinational Monitor* was devoted to exploring the measures and cause of income and wealth inequality in the USA. In July/August, the issue focused on international inequality.

As Edward Wolff described in some write-up, the share of national wealth owned by the richest 1 per cent has doubled during the past three decades. In addition, as Jared Bernstein explains income inequality has skyrocketed nearly as fast. These are startling changes in the relative affluence of the country's population over a very short period. They leave the country more class-bound, less democratic, less just, and more riving by wealth and income inequality gaps that mean people's basic life opportunities are unequal. Most of the increase in wealth created over the last decades has been captured by a small silver of the population.

While the well-off have become better off and the rich have become opulently so, the middle and lower class (groups) have struggled to stay in place. It took until the late 1990s for the inflation-adjusted average wage of the bottom 80 per cent of the population to catch up with the levels of the early 1970s. Wealth of the richest 1 per cent has skyrocketed, while personal and consumer debt has ballooned for those in the middle and lower bottom.

There was nothing inevitable about these trends, and no forces of nature prevented them from being reversed. Rather, the rise in wealth and income inequality is due to shifting power relationships and policy choices favouring the rich, each of which reinforces the other. Capital has grabbed power from labour and corporations have taken power from citizens. The federal government as well as the state and local, have pursued policies, from trade to labour laws, which have strengthened with corporate power and weakened workers. A vicious cycle has ensued with corporations then better positioned to lobby and advocate for still more policy changes to shift income, wealth, and power.

There are too many intertwined factors driving the growth of inequality to identify them all, or to separate out the relative contributions of each, but it is important to pinpoint specific contributing causes. Identifying these factors is a prerequisite to remedying or addressing each, and ultimately to reversing the trends of rising inequality. Focusing on the policies and trends driving inequality is important in order to dispense with the myth that growing inequality is inevitable. To this, it should be enough to cite Edward Wolff pointing out that wealth inequality in the United States actually fell steadily from the period of the Great Depression, until the early or mid-1970s, alternatively, simply the outgrowth of new technologies. Detailing the causes of inequality is also important because it makes clear that many ways in which the recent era of enhanced corporate rule and corporate globalisation have not led to broadly shared benefits, but to modest gains in wealth that have been appropriated by a relative few.

TEN IMPORTANT CONTRIBUTING FACTORS TO SURGING INEQUALITY IN THE UNITED STATES

FALLING LEVELS OF UNIONISATION

Unions now represent less than 10 per cent of the workforce in the private sector in the US. Yet they still represent the single best means for workers to improve their economic conditions. There is a more than 28 per cent wage premium for union membership in the US—meaning that the single fact for belonging to a union raises the average worker's wage more than 28 per cent, and it is far higher in the area of benefits. However, even reference to the dramatic wage premium understates the importance of unions. Unions' power is collective power. When unions represent a higher proportion of the workforce when there is greater union density in a particular industry, unions can raise the overall industry wage rate, including for non-union workers. When unions represent a higher proportion of the national workforces, they can raise the national wage rate.

Even more importantly, when there is greater national union density, unions can exert power that is more political. To ensure the benefits and pain in the national economy is more equally shared. As Kate Bronfenbrenner describes the erosion of the US manufacturing base, vicious anti-union campaigns by employers and inadequate organising efforts by labour has led to the drop-off in union representation in the United States.

THE CORPORATE GLOBALISATION

The corporate globalisation trade regime—manifested in the rules of the World Trade Organization and other trade agreements—has freed corporations to locate production anywhere in the world for sale anywhere in the world. As Jared Bernstein recounts, millions of high-paying manufacturing jobs have been lost in the United States as a result. Workers who remain in the manufacturing sector are forced to compete in the race to the bottom, with union demands for wage gains replaced by employers' demand for wage givebacks. Sometimes the employers really are unable to compete with lower-wage producers in other countries (sometimes they are those lower-wage producers). In some cases, the employers simply use the threat to threat to enhance profitability. Either way, workers' bargaining leverage is dramatically lessened. Workers lose and owners win.

Moreover, the exact same threats are among the most effective at deterring workers from joining unions. Join a union, employers tell workers in the majority of organising campaigns, and we have to close. We just cannot compete if we are burdened by union wages and union bureaucracy. Nowhere is the intertwined nature of the causes of inequality made clearer; corporate globalisation diminishes the union base and workers' power. Weaker unions are less able to defend their jobs, either in direct negotiations with companies or in policymaking disputes in Congress.

DECLINING MINIMUM WAGE

One way to place a floor on the downwards push on wages is to maintain a respectable minimum wage. Because the minimum wage in the United States is set periodically and not pegged to inflation, it is forever losing value, though periodically bumped up a bit when drop gets severe and political momentum makes it hard for Republicans to defeat a minimum wage rise. There has been no progress whatsoever in the obvious solution to this problem, which is to raise the minimum wage and then peg it to the inflation rate so that it rises with the cost of living. Low-wage industries—led by the restaurant association—have led the Chamber of Commerce and the major national business lobbies to oppose minimum wage hikes.

Today the minimum wage of $5.15 has been stuck since 1970. In inflation-adjusted terms, its current value is almost a quarter less than its peak in the late 1960s. In one of the most vibrant economic justice campaigns in the United States today, many communities have passed living wage laws, requiring employers to pay not just a minimum wage, but a minimum wage sufficient to enable a family to survive. Unfortunately, these laws typically apply only to government contractors or sometimes to recipients of government benefits, but not to the overall community. They are an important step forward, and provide some hope for the future, but for now have not managed to have broad nationally felt impacts on wage rate.

SOARING STOCK MARKET

Although the market has come back down to earth to more reasonable levels in the last couple of years, it has grown dramatically over the last three decades. The 'sustainable' part of this stock market rise—meaning stock prices justifiable in relationship to earnings or profits, and the prospect for future profits—reflects spikes of very high profits, including in the mid-1990s. Those high profits themselves were due to a variety of factors. However, among them were the increased reliance on overseas manufacturing and monopolistic markets enabling corporations to impose excessive prices on consumers.

Popular myth to the contrary, the stock market gains accurate overwhelmingly to the rich. Edward Wolff explains that stock holdings are as concentrated now as they were historically.

TAX CUTS FOR THE RICH

Not minding that the federal tax code remains somewhat progressive—meaning higher income earners pay a higher proportion of their income in taxes than lower earners—it is less so than it has been historically. The Reagan administration and Bush second-term tax cuts have massively reduced the tax take from the rich, and the last Bush tax cuts before he left office reduced the level still further. More than a third of the value the Bush proposal gave more to the richest 1 per cent of taxpayers, according to Robert McIntyre of the Citizens for Tax Justice. Nearly half of the benefits went to the richest 50 per cent of taxpayers. However, President Obama wants to change the tax cuts but he would face opposition from the Republican Party as well as some Democrats who enjoy inequality to their benefit.

State taxes, heavily reliant on sales tax, remain regressive, and the current state funding deficit is likely to lead states to increase regressive taxes. The one very important offset in the gloomy tax story has been the earned income tax credit, a federal tax rebate for the lowest income earners that has meaningfully raised the income level of the poorest.

REDUCED TAXES ON CORPORATION

Robert McIntyre explains, thanks to tax code revisions and fancy tax sheltering the corporate share, if paid federal taxes are down to approximately 7 per cent compared to 22 per cent level in the 1960s.

DECLINING WELFARE PAYMENTS TO THE POOR, INCREASED PAYMENT TO THE RICH

The last three decades have seen a steady decline in traditional welfare payments to the poor, leaving them considerably worse off—though again this condition has been considerably offset by the earned income tax credit. At the same time as they have cut welfare for the poor, local, state, and federal governments have become far more generous in making gifts to the corporate welfare kings. To take two indicators: In the period from 1970s to the 1990s, corporate bailout has grown from the level of hundreds of millions of dollars to hundreds of billions of dollars.

The defence budget, which serves corporate welfare as much as any other purpose, has soared under the Reagan and second Bush administration, a simple transfer from taxpayers to Lockheed, Boeing, Raytheon, and their shareholders.

AN OUT-OF-WHACK FINANCIAL SYSTEM

The banking system systematically deprives lower income and minority communities of the credit they need to build up investment and wealth. The services that provided become increasingly shady, in addition to price-gouging check cashing operation, and payday under. Meanwhile, the super-aggressive marketing of credit cards to middle-income people has led many to fall deeper into debt and forced them to pay off huge accumulated debts at serious interest rates.

Also in Western Europe, such as in Spain over the last six years, estate agents in collaboration with banks exploited immigrants, granting them enormous credit to buy houses, with a criminal intent. Banks granted loans to people while in the process enriching themselves and estate agents to the detriment of the clients. In the Netherlands for example, as an immigrant, you are never granted loans to invest in your native country unless you are going to invest in Dutch society; you can never get loans from the bank to develop yourself. I believe these policies limit the poor immigrants from developing and improving their living standards.

TIGHT MONEY FROM THE FEDERAL RESERVE

Although it has loosened its grip on the money supply in recent years, at crucial periods over the last three decades, the Fed has driven up interest rates and plunged the economy in recession. The resultant high unemployment rates diminished workers' power and pushed down wages.

A CULTURE OF OVERCOMPENSATION AND ACCEPTANCE OF THE WEALTH DIVIDE

Though the continued routine of obscenely high executive pay directly affects few people to meaningfully affect overall income inequality, it has created a culture in which professionals and people in upper-income groups are expected to be paid very generously. New class-based social norms have emerged about what constitutes a reasonable salary, and how much a person 'needs' to get by. What upper-income groups view as necessity is, of course, unavailable to most people in the country.

This culture, nurtured by new marketing campaigns advertising luxurious lifestyles and media that more and more narrowly target upper-income groups, has helped push up salaries broadly at the top. However, these riches are not available to all. Part of the culture has been the normalisation and acceptance of a persistent and deepening income and wealth inequality, with the situation of middle- and lower-income groups largely absent from the news or popular culture.

Recently we have seen the emergence of greed among the financial institutions and bank CEOs rearing its ugly head again, after bailout by the poor taxpayers' money to stay afloat, from all the federal governments in Asia, Europe, and the United States. They have appropriated again large sums of money in executive pay for themselves while the poor people continue to lose their homes and suffer economically. The upper class continue to be richer, and the poor continue in the track of poverty. Just in five months, these greedy people that lack conscience have taken compensation running into hundreds of millions, if not billions for themselves and families while we live without hope of escape from the mess they created.

On 30 July 2009 in the US, both Houses passed bills 237 and 185 to limit executive compensation. Though the Republican Party are critical about it, the bill will pass so that these crooks can be put in check before the silence of the masses will break, because if it did, there will be mass attack on the super rich soon. In addition, we need moderation in the way we live, to avoid another crisis. People who are unable to pay loans should not be given big loans or credit cards. This makes inequality increase and continues to haunt the poor, who suffer most, while creating more money for the rich.

EFFECTS OF RACE ON INCOME AND WEALTH INEQUALITY IN THE US

It is easy to deny or accuse others of racism, which is also obvious that it exists, whether white racism or black racism. Both black and white practice racism in one way or another, but the question remains why it is used to fashion the society we live in. One race has played a dominant role against the others in order to benefit its kind. This is not right, but it has been happening for over 400–500 years of American history, and I believe the time has come for us to search our souls and say what is wrong is wrong, no matter who is involved.

However, it is not only in America that race is a factor; it is everywhere: Europe, Africa, Asia, and the Middle East. Many have limited the success and progress of others because of racial inequality. Income and wealth in the United States has been unequal because of racial inequality practice in US. Sometimes, we might think that race issue in America directed only against black Americans, because in the early 1940s to 1950s, Jews were also discriminated against, but they were able to overcome the prejudice directed against them by those of white European descent in the US.

Because one cannot hide his physical appearance, the burden of racial inequality falls more on blacks than on other races around the world. Blacks have become the target of everyone who wants to see who he or she is better than; even a dumb and illiterate white person thinks he or she is better than even the most intelligent black. Moreover, the idea of the whites to continue to dominate everywhere continues to create and paint a negative image of black people, which hinders them from having equal opportunity with them, though some black people's attitude does create room for questioning the moral and ethical values they lack to live in an integrated society. Most of them refuse to embrace change which can empower them to change their condition.

The story of Dr Philip Emeagwali, a Nigerian-born US citizen, once a Gordon Bell Prize winner, was his experience of how racist American and white society is when it comes to relations with blacks. He was limited over the years in the field of science until he could no longer be stopped from having his breakthrough that earned him the Gordon Bell Prize; this is an example of the race issue we talk about every day, though many deny its existence.

Income is what the average American family used to reproduce daily existence in the form of shelter, food, clothing, and other necessities. While wealth is a storehouse of resources, it is what families own and use to reproduce income. It is an established fact that there are income and wealth inequalities in America, though the income of racial minorities has increased in the recent years. But the gap between minorities and whites remains. It suggested that various races are competing in somewhat level playing field; it challenged when wealth is taken into account.

Dating to the beginning of the slavery days, governmental policies prohibited blacks from beginning businesses. Federal housing authorities made it difficult for African Americans to obtain loans and mortgages. While racial and ethnic minorities were legally denied opportunities to accumulate wealth for future generations, most whites did not encounter these same obstacles. Perpetuations of these practices for centuries attest to the wide wealth inequalities among whites and minorities. Because home ownership plays such a large role in wealth portfolios of American families, it is a prime source of the differences between black and white net worth. Home ownership rates for blacks are 20 per cent lower than rates for whites; hence, blacks possess less of this important source of equity.

Thomas Shapiro uses the concept of transformative assets to explain racial inequality in wealth in United States. Transformative assets mean inherited wealth from previous generations that lift families beyond their own achievement. Inheritance is important right now because the generation that benefited from the post–World War II economic boom is now at the age when they are passing on their wealth to their children. Shapiro says that these assets help white people more than they helped black people. This means that whites have more wealth and head-start assets than blacks do. It is a crucial cause of disparity between African Americans and whites concerning wealth, because inheritance is the key determinant in what kind of life families enjoy.

There is also a wealth gap between blacks and whites of similar income, similar levels of education, and similar job quality. In all comparisons, black families have less wealth than white families. The imbalance in transformative assets has led to racial inequality between blacks and whites. When whites want to buy houses to settle down, they have less debt because they are more likely to get help from their parents for their college expenses. Many white families rely on transformative assets rather than their savings, so when they want buy houses, banks grant them lower interest rates, since they are able to make down payment, but blacks rely on their savings, therefore obtaining higher interest rate from banks to buy homes. In addition, the segregation attitude of whites makes black communities disadvantaged areas for investment, with their perception that black communities are prone to crime and violence.

A huge implication of segregation of communities that results from inequality in wealth is inequality in education. Housing discrimination and the effects of transformative assets limit educational progress. Communities with better home values receive more funding for schools.

This results in better-quality schools in primarily white suburban communities, while primarily black and Hispanic communities in the inner cities do not receive adequate funding or government attention.

Adding to the ever-growing gap between white and black Americans is their weekly earnings. In1981, black males averaged a week income that was approximately 20 per cent below that of white males. In addition, not only are black males not paid the same as white males, they are also more likely to experience unemployment. In 1980, black males on average were over 60 per cent more likely to endure unemployment. In addition, their time on unemployment is 30 per cent longer than that of white males. These statistical numbers are also not expected to change any time soon. Research showed that from the years 1948 to 1997, the racial income gap was closing at annual rate of 0.4 per cent.

Many studies have shown that earnings do not increase with job experience for black males as they do for white males. These studies have also shown that black males are hired for jobs that have few promotional benefits. On the other hand, white males accept jobs with training requirements to receive promotions and pay raises. In brief, white males receive jobs with promotional incentives, and blacks simply do not. Studies have also shown that even when both black and white have the same level of education, their income still differs, with whites receiving more than blacks do. In 1960, white males received $700 more than blacks with same level of education (less than elementary education) and those with diploma $1,400 more than blacks do.

This shows how unequal America is in wealth, income, education, and other areas of societal living. The disparities exist in every corner of the society. You sometimes hear the white people say that blacks are lazy, they do not want to work; but in fact, these factors can discourage men if they do not think very well and are not strong enough to accept it as they see it. In addition, it pushes them more to crime where they think they can make easy and quick money. However, education is one of the means to escape this inequality in the unequal society we are living in.

POVERTY AND INEQUALITY
IN A GLOBAL SCALE

It is a well-known fact even to the learned and unlearned that there is inequality of income and wealth globally. Many nations are living and flourishing in affluence/wealth where others live in abject poverty that is incomparable on any scale. In the United States and many European countries, whites spend more money on their pets than some families can afford to feed in a day or month.

Capitalism is hundreds of years old and today dominates nearly every part of the globe. Its champions claim it is the greatest engine of production growth the world has ever seen. They also argue that it is unique in its ability to raise the standard of living of every person on earth. Because of capitalism, we are slouching towards utopia—the phrase coined by the University of California at Berkeley economist J. Bradford Delong—slowly but surely heading towards a world in which everyone will have achieved a US style of middle-class life.

The United States is often referred to as a nation dominated by the middle class and one in which it is relatively easy for a poor person to become a person of means. Here, it's said, equality of opportunity rules. It is hard to know what middle class and equality of opportunity means, but it is fair to think that such a society ought to be one in which people do indeed have a great deal of economic mobility. The data on poverty and inequality of income and wealth do not square very well with this image. In the United States, the federal government defined a poverty level of income 'one below which families are defined as poor'. It is an income below which families would find it difficult to live without serious problems and which would place real danger when faced with any sort of economic crisis, such as a sick child or an injury at work. This official poverty level of income is equal to three times the minimum food budget calculated by the Department of Agriculture, a very modest standard with numerous restrictive and unrealistic assumptions put into it, for example, that those poor families will be able to buy food at the lowest unit price and will know how to convert the cheapest food into nutritious meals. In 2002, this was $18.392 for a family of four or 12.1 per cent of the population.

The incidence of poverty was 24 per cent for blacks and 21.8 per cent for Hispanics. In 2002, 35.2 per cent of black children under the age of six lived in poverty, as did 29.1 per cent of Hispanic children. In the United States in 2000, income inequality was greater than at any time since the 1920s, with the richest 5 per cent of all households receiving six times more income than the poorest 20 per cent of households, up from about four times in 1970. According to Paul Krugman in the *New York Times*, perhaps as much as 70 per cent of all the income growth in the United States during 1980s went to the richest 1 per cent of all families. With respect to wealth, in the United States in 1995, the richest 1 per cent of all households owned 42.2 per cent of all stocks, 55.5 per cent of all bonds, 44.2 per cent of all trusts, 71.4 per cent of all non-corporate businesses and 36.9 per cent of all non-home real estate. As with income inequality, this has been increasing at least for the past twenty years or more.

There is no evidence that the high poverty level, income, and wealth inequality is going to be eliminated or reduced in this present society we live in. Great and growing inequality mocks the notion of equality of opportunity. If we consider two children, one born to parents who are rich and influential and another born to a single mother working at night, with three children to care for, which of the two mothers will have the best health care and regular visits to the doctor, means if needed, and healthy diet? Which of the two women's children is more likely to get better/adequate nutrition, best education, and best social class to meet with? If the two children from these two different parents get sick in the middle of the night, which one will be more likely to make it to the emergency room in time? When these two children face the labour market (of course the rich child will never have to face the labour market in the sense the poor child will), which one will be more productive? Automatically the child from a rich mother.

Poverty and inequality themselves generate many socially undesirable outcomes, such as conflict and tension, hatred, and prejudice. If you compare two different countries, one with greater income inequality and the other with less income inequality, there is a tendency for social unrest in the one with greater income inequality than the ones with less income inequality.

Great and growing inequality saps the political power of these people at the bottom, making it more likely that the social welfare programs which help to alleviate the harmful consequences of poverty will be gutted, while at same time making it more likely that policies which further favour the rich will be put in place. The poor are increasingly filled with hopelessness and despair as they contemplate the yawning gap between them and those at the top.

Although there is great poverty and inequality in the richest capitalist country, this cannot compare to the levels of both of these to find in the vast majority of the world's economies, which are both capitalist and poor. The World Bank estimates the number of persons in different countries and in the world as a whole who subsist on less than $1 and $2 per day. In Nigeria, for example, in the early 1990s, 90.8 per cent of the population lived on $2 per day or less. In India, the figure was 86.2 per cent in 1997. In a world population of some 6 billion persons, the World Bank estimates that 2.8 billion survive on $2 per day or less (about 45 per cent per day or less). Also, the World Bank compares the numbers in these countries with those of the United States poverty level of income. In 2002, the income level in United States was $12.60 per day per person, and those poor countries are now a little more than $1 per day.

Poverty on a global scale is matched by an enormous and growing inequality of incomes, a fact remarked upon in considerable detail in the November 2002 review of the month in a magazine. In China and India, the world's most populous nations and two of its fastest growing economies, inequality is growing rapidly. In China, once an extremely egalitarian country, income inequality is now barely distinguishable from that of the United States. China has witnessed perhaps the greatest income redistribution in history. In India, most of the benefits of rapid economic growth are going to the wealthiest 20 per cent of society there, 350 million [persons]—more than a third of the population—live in dire poverty. In Calcutta alone, an estimated 250,000 children sleep on the sidewalks. Recently, the BBC announced that about 250 million are facing starvation and hunger in India.

World Bank economist Branko Milanovic has overseen the most sophisticated attempt to measure income inequality worldwide. Using a massive household survey covering the entire world, he found that the richest 12 per cent of people in the world get as much income as the poorest 57 per cent. The richest 5 per cent had in 1993 an average income 114 times greater than that of the poorest 5 per cent, rising from 78 times in 1988. The poorest 5 per cent grew poorer, losing 25 per cent of their real income growth, while the richest 20 per cent saw their real income grow by 12 per cent more than twice as high as average world income. World inequality grew because inequality grew between and within countries. The rich nations grew richer and the poor nations grew poorer; the rich within each country grew richer at the expense of the poor.

Today, a lot of social movements against globalisation and policies of rich countries against the developing countries are in existence just like the ones we saw during the early revolution as seen in Russia, France, South American countries, and Africa that toppled governments may be in the offing again. Every international conference such as G8 or G20 has witnessed demonstration by social movements against poverty and for debts cancellation for poor countries. One day, it is going to go beyond ordinary demonstration and plummet into serious chaos. It is impossible to tell how all of this 'primitive' and more conscious protest will play out. However, one gets the feeling that political struggle in the coming decades might be intimately tied to the glaring and unconscionable inequality which has become the hallmark of contemporary capitalism. Under these conditions, the system is unlikely to be entirely successful at keeping the lid on the boiling discontent underneath.

CHAPTER 5

Religious Inequality

Religion is part of the human society and will continue to be, irrespective of different opinions about its role in the society we live in. Many profess different religions, be it Christianity, Islam, Judaism, Hinduism, Buddhism, Animism, Confucianism, and many others. In most countries around the globe, religion has played a part in shaping the society, either in a positive or negative way. Constitutions of many nations have been born out of religion or faith. Many constitution-guiding nations took their roots from the religion the nation believes in, but still many blame religion as a contributing factor in conflicts around the world. Some one may ask, what is religion?

Religion is that which offers guidance for conduct both in public and private life amid changing cultures and lifestyles; thus, it both influences and assimilates the characteristics of the culture it is associated with. Spirituality, on the other hand, as we understand is a faith commitment that is not necessarily linked to a particular religious tradition or institution. In fact, religion is not and will not be a contributor to violence and conflict, but the people are the factor for violence and conflict in religion. All religions, I believe, preaches love and harmony if there is no other thing they have in common, but do we the people practice this principle? Jesus Christ, the founder of Christian religion, said, 'You have heard that it was said, "Love your friends and hate your enemies." Now I tell you, love your enemies and pray for those who persecute you. So you will become the children of your father in heaven. For he makes, his sun shine on bad and good people alike and gives rain to those who do well and to those who do evil. Why should Jehovah reward you if you love only those who love you? What man is Jesus Christ to you then, that his religion does not preach violence hatred and division with this idea. Therefore, if you hate and cause violence in the name of Christianity you are not Christ like and should blame not Christian religion for your fault.' Mathew 5:45–48. I remember what Gandhi told the British Empire in India saying, 'If we all can be able to do what Jesus Christ preached on the Sermon on the Mount, we would be able to solve half of the world's problems including those of mine and yours.'

Islamic religion says that he who saves one man has saved the whole humanity, and he who destroys one has destroyed the whole humanity. So if an Islamic fanatic kills and claims that he is doing it in the name of Islam, he is lying and such brings discredit to the religion. The religion is not violence, divisiveness, tension, or conflict. We, the people are who hide behind religion to create inequality in society filled with all dirty ideas and philosophies that have no moral standing.

Religion has created a lot of tension, inequality, conflict, and wars in the past and continues to create until now by those who use it as a means to an end for their selfish objectives. The great crusades by Muslim or Christian crusaders were born out of people's selfish ambitious adventure than it is about the religion itself. There are many factions today within many religions. In Islam, you have the Shiite, Sunnis, and others. In Christianity, you have the Catholics, Protestants, Pentecostals, and a host of others; in Judaism, you have the Orthodox and real Orthodox, and other sects. All these religious divide goes with its self-created tension and conflicts associated with it due to man's insatiable desire for perfection of their own not of the religion.

The oldest Christian conflict exists today in Western Europe where the inequality that exists between the Catholic believers and Protestant believers has remained unsolved, irrespective of all peace efforts to reconcile these two sides who say they are Christians or 'Christlike'. To be frank they are not like Christ, who represents love and forgiveness, who came to reconcile humankind with God despite man's disobedience. So let the people of Northern Ireland go and read the Bible and apply the word of the religion they profess. So let no man blame Christianity for such conflict; you have to blame the people who have refused to purge their hearts of inequality and hatred. Everywhere around the globe today, you hear about the daily attacks of Muslims against their fellow brothers only because they are Christians, from Nigeria to India, Iraq to Pakistan, just to mention a few. Even the Jews and Hindus are not left out of the regular attacks by those who claim to be Muslims. In addition, their fellow Muslims are not left out of their anger, where Sunnis attack Shiites, and Shiites against Sunnis—the story never ends.

The dominant attitude of one religion against the other fuels resentments, tension, and unequal treatment against people who may have different meaning or belief. In fact, people have used religion to promote and practice inequality of all sorts against their fellow creation of God. However, it is practical that when people are unequally treated, they have legitimate right to resent it, and is human nature to do so. I believe religion should be a healing and bridge-building factor among people rather than separating them. The story and history of the Pilgrim Fathers also show how people can manipulate religion to serve their selfish ambition and interest, and we can possibly blame it on religion. The Pilgrim Fathers or the separatists with their associated inequality attitude originated in England before they moved to the United States in September of 1620. They left England in 1607-08 for the Netherlands where they settled before moving to the United States. During the tension and conflict between the Catholic and the Protestant, the separatists left for the Netherlands to search for religious tolerance that existed there. However, due to their attitude of being God's elect as they claimed to be, they could not live in the Netherlands because of the Dutch's loose morals, so they decided to move in 1620. When they arrived in Plymouth, Massachusetts in a dead winter, the Native Americans welcomed them and assisted them, taught them how to grow native crops. Nevertheless, when they became rich, they turned against their host with attitude of inequality and racism, which still rule in the United States until to date. If you have different meaning from them, you are branded evil or declared to have come from the devil and therefore you could end up being burned at the stake.

TO WHAT EXTENT HAS RELIGION CONTRIBUTED TO EITHER THE PERPETUATION OR ERADICATION OF INEQUALITY?

Is it as Marx contended the 'Opiate of the Masses' or might it be as evidenced in liberation theology, the catalyst for social change? Over the past two decades, Pope John Paul II (late) has assailed the inequalities between developed and developing nations. In Durango, Mexico in 1990, for instance, he argued that capitalism had neglected its ethical responsibilities, and he challenged industrialized countries and big businesses to stop 'hoarding and to start distributing wealth fairly' the excessive hoarding of riches by some and which are denied from the majority. Thus, the very wealth that is accummulated generates poverty. In 1986, the American Roman Catholic bishops adopted a pastoral letter proclaiming that poverty levels in the United States were a 'social and moral scandal' and stated that the US government must do more to create jobs and help the poor.

When thinking about the civic activities of religious faith, what undoubtedly comes to mind are their charity programs for the poor. Indeed, among the arguments heard in the dismantling of welfare state is how churches and established charities are more effective and efficient in their aid to the less fortunate. In addition, there is the influence of churches upon the civic motivations of their members. In an analysis of American Volunteers, using the results of the 1996 NORC General Social Survey, it was found that strongly religious individuals were significantly more likely to have volunteered for two or more causes, 45 per cent more than those not very religious or having no religious affiliation (27 per cent). Among the religious faiths, Jews (44 per cent) are most likely to be high volunteers, followed by Liberal Protestants (41 per cent), moderate Protestants (39 per cent), fundamentalist

Protestants (33 per cent), and Catholics (29 per cent). On the other hand, religion and religious people were found to have weak or non-existent relationships with attributions of the poor and attitudes towards whether the government should do something to reduce inequalities between the rich and poor. When NORC interviewers asked Americans in 1996 if they or any members of their household had given food or clothing to the homeless or street people, they found the following results:

Percentage of respondents saying they have given to the homeless according to religious faiths and religiosity

	Strong	Somewhat	Not very	Total
Fundamental Protestant	37%	47%	33%	37%
Catholics	40%	45%	41%	41%
Liberal Protestant	42%	37%	31%	35%
Moderate Protestant	40%	29%	29%	33%
Non Affiliation				36%
Total	39%	40%	35%	38%

RELIGION'S ROLE IN MAINTAINING INEQUALITY

Religion is an excellent stuff for keeping common people quiet (Napoleon Bonaparte, 1769 -1821. The idea of God has never bound the whole individual to society but has always bound the oppressed classes by a belief in the divinity of the oppressors. (Lenin of Russian Bolsheviks)

Arthur Schlesinger, in *The Cycles of American History* (1986), observed that 'the great religious ages were notable for their indifference to human rights in the contemporary sensenot only for their acquiescence in poverty, inequality, and oppression, but for their enthusiastic justification of slavery, persecution, torture, and genocide.' The case of the 1994 genocide in Rwanda also shows how religion has aided and played part in inequality. When Christians look beyond religion and faith in Christ and supported the killing of the innocent because of tribal tradition, inequality proves beyond reasonable doubt what Schlesinger is talking about.

The war in Bosnia was also a case of religion playing a part in unequal treatment because of differences in belief. The Bosnia Muslims were murdered in great number by Christians who lived in that land. The idea of inequality in faith was paramount in the Bosnia war where people were tortured, persecuted, and killed. The case of Islamic crusaders who rampaged Northern Africa in AD 630–706, spreading violence in order to prove the superiority of their religion, and the forced conversion to Islam of non-Muslims who were then killed, were all done in the name of religion. Millions were persecuted, tortured, and killed during the Ottoman Empire's Islamic ruthlessness against non-Muslims. Also during the early centuries, Jews were persecuted for refusing to become Christians. Be it in Spain, Italy, France, many Jews were burnt or hanged because of religious inequality posed by the then Christians. However, Martin Luther was against it. He said that Jews can be converted to Christianity if Christians can treat them and show them the love of Christ Jesus who created all men equal.

DOES RELIGIOSITY INCREASE THE LIKELIHOOD OF BEING HAPPY FOR THOSE AT THE LOWER RUNG OF THE STRATIFICATION ORDER?

Results (combined 1973–1994) General Social Survey

Percentage of people who are very happy by religiosity and self-identified social class

Class	Lower N=1,327	Working N=12,113	Middle N=12,247	Upper N=831	Total
Strong	22%	34%	44%	53%	39%
Somewhat	15%	28%	36%	48%	32%
Not Very	13%	24%	33%	46%	28%
No Affilit Ns	13%	24%	31%	31%	24%
Total	16%	28%	38%	48%	33%

Religiosity and stratification (social stratification)

Equality and fairness to all people–that is what we need in the human society be it religious or otherwise.

RELIGION'S ROLE IN MAINTAINING INEQUALITY

Religious belief can reinforce wealth inequalities. The poor will tend to stay poor and the rich will tend to remain rich—either way, religion has a significant effect on the level of persistence in a given socioeconomic constituency. The theology of your church may be justifying and contributing to socioeconomic inequalities rather than helping to solve it. This is my initial thought and I want to explain it a bit. Many churches today have turned themselves into financial institutions or banks where they think you invest or keep your money. Followers of many Christian religions have been ripped off by their church doctrines of tithe or tithing, where they tell the poor to invest and God will reward them back in millionfold. Through this process, the poor people pay money to enrich the men of God while the people continue in poverty without help from the church. They make the poor to become poorer, while the men of God's wallet continues to grow bigger and richer.

The men of God and churches have forgotten the word of God in Mathew 6:33, 'Seek first the Kingdom of God and every other thing shall be added unto you.' Now, they are seeking riches instead of the kingdom. They extort money from poor believers with threatening messages that God will curse you if you withhold your tithes. Nevertheless, this is not scriptural because God never said he would bless you if you pay tithe, but he said if you obey his words, there are blessings attached to it. The church has gone astray like a shepherdless sheep; they now seek prosperity and material wealth instead of saving souls. You all hear the doctrine of sowing seed today in cash, give your money to the church, and reap the reward tomorrow; whether you are a sinner or not, what is important is the money you give. Please tell these churches to read Acts 20, 1 Peter 5, Galatians 6:2, 1 Timothy 6.

Religion is not for personal gains as the men of God have turned it to be in recent years. The church has become the richest empire today, supporting and practicing inequality. Sometimes if you are not rich, you cannot earn a special place in church; but when you are rich, you earn titles in the church, such as as deacon, elder, knight, and others.

What is a church? Paul used the metaphor of the body of Christ in his first letter to the Corinthians. However, God has so arranged the body, giving the greater honour to the inferior members, that there may be no dissension within the body, but the members may have the same care for one another. If one member suffers, all suffer together with it; if one member is honoured, all rejoice together with it. Now you are the body of Christ and individual members of it. 1 Corinthians 12:12–26.

The church is made up of people who believe in the saving power of a risen Lord. It is the church, which has received this saving power to act as the physical representative of the living Lord. The church is that physical entity which is not only a symbol of the saving power of Christ but is the very means by which God continues to enact and perform acts of grace and love in the world.

God was incarnate in Christ Jesus and now God is incarnate in the church, which is you and I. In Christ, God reconciled the world that had missed the mark and needed to turn back to the true God, as had been the case in so many instances in the past. However, Paul does not believe that this work of reconciliation, the very work of God in Christ, was done in vain. 'God is making his appeal through us' as a continual act of reconciliation. So where is the seat of this continuing activity of God to reconcile the world? It is the body of Christ, which is the church. The church is therefore a communion of ambassadors and representatives of the kingdom of God on earth. It is the job of the church to have its feet firmly planted in the contingent whims of a suffering world, the world that resides in eternity. The church is the bridge to perfection in God.

The question is how many people today in church understand their role in this regard and what it actually entails? It is clearly about public displays of piety and massive light shows to attract people in the buildings, to raise funds to maintain the buildings and men of God, to attract more people to come in the door. So if not, then what? To whom did Jesus Christ minister? Who actually listened to him when he spoke of forgiveness and love? Who truly received his message of accountability and judgement? Many were proud of their beliefs and status among the people of God, such as the fishermen, tax collectors, prostitutes, lame, blind, lepers, and vile people of the society. These are the ones heard and believed and who truly received his reconciliation. These people understood that Jesus Christ was there to reconcile them with God and make things right in their lives. They knew it will not come without a price, but the dividend will be seen not with their eyes, but with their heart, minds, and soul invaded and purchased with the blood of God love for them. Jesus Christ did not condemn those he saved; he simply fed them and they ate.

Jesus Christ disrupted the boundaries of the order of his time. He revealed the tentativeness and fragility of the structures that people had established. With Christ Jesus, there were no safety nets that humans can construct. How well does the body of Christ live up to this standard? How often do we freely welcome outcasts and sinners of this world? Do we condemn them before they are allowed into the holy of holies? Do we tell them, they may break bread with us but only if they adhere to certain conditions of our fragile laws and weak apprehension of God is reconciling act through us?

The church today and some time in the past has become of the world and legitimizes the things that Jesus Christ disrupted, including inequality of wealth among its members. It legitimizes inequalities and suffering. Also, we would venture a good guess that it also legitimizes mediocrity and comfort. If the church is the means for God to enact this work of reconciliation in the world, who is reconciled and how is the church doing this work? As affiliation and members shift in the United States and around the globe, perhaps more mirrors are needed in our churches. Look at yourself in the mirror as you pray. Is the image you see in front of you an icon of God's work of reconciliation in the world, or do you see an idol of the things of the world that legitimates division, inequality, and mediocrity (from Drew Tatuska).

EFFECTS OF RELIGION ON WEALTH INEQUALITY

Kesters observed that Christian theology might be contributing and justifying socioeconomic inequality rather than helping to solve it. Kester says that a typical conservative protestant 'might be a member of the Assemblies of God, Church of Christ, Nazarene, and Pentecostal churches'. According to Kesters's article in the *American Journal of Sociology* 'Conservative Protestants and Wealth: How Religion Perpetuates Assets Poverty', he argues that traditional views of money— it is God's not ours—keep many Protestants from building financial safety nets. While some struggle to build up their banks accounts, others like Anne Thompson of Louisville, Kentucky, chooses to give it all away in order to pursue what they see as God's plan for their lives.

Some study has demonstrated that religion affects wealth indirectly through educational attainment, fertility, and female labour force participation. The results also provide evidence of the direct effect of religion on wealth. Low rates assets accumulation and unique economic values combine to reduce CP (Conservative Protestant) wealth beyond the effects of demography. The findings improve the understanding of the relationship between religious beliefs and inequality. The primary effects of religious beliefs found in the notion that all property is God's is reinforced by inherency in the religious group that Kesters studied. Some of the largely and more widely recognized CP denominations are Baptist, Church of Christ, Assemblies of God, Pentecostal, and Nazarene. At least 25 per cent of the United States population belong to some CP denominations.

Conservative ideas of religion mediate the relationship between wealth and religion, and contribute to low income in conservative households. It also affects wealth behaviour over time. CP also seems to seek divine guidance in making financial and work decisions, and they avoid accumulation of wealth. For instance, Anne Thompson, forty-three years old, gave up a six-figure salary in 2002 and quit her job to follow God's call to impact popular culture Christian message. She said goodbye to plans for early retirement and her $800,000 house and has not received a paycheck since. To be sure, her above-average means put her in a higher- than-average income bracket, but her motivations are not much different from many other conservative Protestants. Thompson believes using her money to answer God's call is more important than using it for herself, even if her current financial situation is a 'mere shadow' of what it once was. 'Words can hardly describe the life that comes in return for whatever it is that you are sacrificing,' said Thompson, who describes herself as a conservative Protestant, 'in my case it happened to be financial.'

Finally, and perhaps most importantly, these findings have significant implications for understanding inequality in the United States, and inequality in a comparative perspective. The starting point for the study was the observation that wealth inequality is extreme in the United States and the supposition that religion may have some influence on the level of inequality. While Kesters did not study inequality directly, his findings do suggest that CPS—a large segment of American population—began to accumulate wealth more like other groups. We might find out that wealth inequality was reduced. Future research might explore this issue more directly using simulation models to understand how changing savings behaviour for CPS affects wealth distribution. In addition, the United States has distinctive high levels of inequality and high levels of religiosity. It is possible that inequality at least is particularly explained by religiosity among both CPS and other religious groups that are chronically poor. Arthur Schlesinger Sr. once observed that democracy in the United States has become the 'government of the corporations, by the corporations, and for the corporations'. How can it be saved from cynicism that inevitably erodes people's fundamental confidence in democratic institutions? The church seems to have largely abandoned its prophetic office with reference to the American economic policy, the reason for which is unclear. Is it because many religious groups are too preoccupied with sexuality, sexual misconduct, or other issues of individual morality or their own institutional survival? Or you may ask have the churches allowed their own financial interest to compromise them? What is clear is that this compelling and provocative idea has much to say to religious leaders concerned about the integrity of democracy in America and about the integrity of the church in its public commitments.

Presidents such as Andrew Jackson (1830), Theodore Roosevelt and Franklin D. Roosevelt's New Deal, the proposed economic reforms that will reduce inequality in the society are a thing that we need today. Now former president Obama wanted to run a policy that will reduce inequality in the United States and the Republican Christians and blue Dog Democrats Christians as well are branding it as socialism. And if so, is socialism a disease more than capitalism? In a country so rich and ranked first in religiosity, and one that promotes love, care, and sharing equally, here many are against healthcare reform, which will reduce inequality in health and alleviate people's suffering that is long overdue.

It is an amazing but true story. There are still people who put the kingdom first before materialism. Many Christians today are the so-called political leaders who preach and design policy of inequality in both religion and political agenda. Many Christian political parties in Europe in the recent years have become anti-immigrant in order to win the elections. They fear men instead of God. They support agendas that create inequality against migrants and those that have different meaning or opinion from them. Rome, the centre of Christendom, has destroyed homes of migrants from Romania (Gypsies) without you hearing any opposing voice from Christians around the world. Many African migrants have be assassinated in broad daylight in the streets of Rome, with no one paying a price for that. Why? Because the value of the lives of European Christians are different from that of Africans. Last time, an immigrant family from Afghanistan was discovered in Italy living in an abandoned sewerage system because they were trying to hide from Italian police and immigration agents of Berlusconi in a Christian country with dirty inequality attitude.

Today the inequality meted out against Christian Sudanese in the South has been ignored by their fellow brothers and sisters in Christ be it those in Africa, Asia, Europe, and the United States. They only shouted for the head of Omar Bashir but never did a damn thing to get it. Their interest in oil overshadowed their love for fellow believers. Once Muslims practice inequality against Christians you will never hear them cry foul, but once a Christian does that against them then heaven will get loose, brother. Most of the time, Christian-Muslim apologists are defending and rationalizing the situation. Hey! Wake up, man, and think.

IS IT FOR RELIGION TO ENSHRINE INEQUALITY?

So why cannot the world's big religion get it. There was news that clergy members have written to the Archbishop of Canterbury and York to say they will leave the Church of England if women bishops are ordained. Priest. The 1,300 clergymen, which include several bishops, also want to have exemption from serving under them, but excuse me for asking what their problem is? In this one those areas where the great and the good from the Church of England will quote the teachings of the Bible, or is that just religious chaff, smoke and mirrors, to hide bad, old-fashioned sexism? Why would a female bishop be any less good at being a bishop than her opposite (male) number.

Judaism too insists that men and women have very different roles in both the place of worship, and within a framework of social structure—and how that in itself is a function of the religion. Is that fair? Why don't Jewish women just say *enough!*? The Jewish prayer book uses 'our' in prayers and some other faiths would use 'I' and 'mine'. How can religion that tries to be so inclusive, even down to its use of language, be excluding when it comes to women? On the other hand, am I missing something here?

Islam too has distinct attitudes towards women. It is a tricky relationship between women and Islam defined by both Islamic texts and the history and culture of the Muslim world. Sharia law provides for difference between women's and men's roles and their rights. Muslim-majority countries have given women varying degrees of rights concerning marriage, divorce, civil rights, legal status, dress code, and education. In Islam, women and men cannot worship in the same mosque at the same time. Women are excluded from men's areas of prayers, yet the same men sleep with the same women in their respective homes; but in the mosque, inequality is practiced against women. If religion equals tribe minus the trappings of religion, can the idea of being a citizen in your church, synagogue, or mosque co-exist with being a woman? Let alone being a woman at the top of the religious tree. Why can't the big religions be courageous enough to reform? Do they need to reform too? Why not just leave them the way they are, with a free get out of jail card when it comes to women and what they can do and cannot do. (from BBC)

WHY COMMUNISTS MUST FIGHT RELIGION

Communists fight for the working class. Workers cannot be free of exploitation and the miseries of capitalism until they have overthrown the ruling classes and run society by themselves. Comments have always studied the class struggles of the past and this study shows that workers must organize under a party that fights for their interest and that will never sell out to the Bosses—a communist party. Violent revolution is necessary since no ruling class yields power without a violent struggle.

Communists said that the people must oppose religion because religion is always and everywhere a tool of the rulers to dominate the workers. Religion is essentially elitist and undemocratic. Communist is materialists; we must use science to unmask false ideas. Throughout the ages, nothing has heeded back the struggle of the exploit for justice and nothing has caused us much passivity as religion. We encourage all comrades and friends to critique this message to write further articles exposing how religion keeps oppressing all of us and serves the Bosses.

However, in Stalin's idea and perception about religion as you look at it presently and in the past, there are elements of truth in what he is saying. Religion has achieved a lot in history in helping people out of inequality, but at times also, people to maintain and support inequality have used it. Religion should be about love, care, charity, and harmony, but when people use it as a tool to disfranchise people, discriminate and dominate, then there is reason for someone to oppose and criticize it. Today, many who abuse religion for their own benefit always say, 'Touch not my anointed and do my prophet no harm.' If the anointed and prophet of God is living under the laws of God and in obedience to it, nobody will touch you or harm you. However, if you disrupt the rules of Jehovah, you will be touched and harmed. If the anointed practices inequality, preach hatred, rob people of their money with good lies and sow seed of division and violence surely he will be touched or harmed either by Jehovah or by man, irrespective of the type of religion that used to keep the people silent when they are supposed to speak. God is love and religion should embody that love and not otherwise. The use of religion to perpetuate inequality and create violence should end, instead of people hiding behind religion to propagate their evil desires. They should come out and let religion be, because on its own, it is not violence.

RELIGION AND ECONOMY

The Hindutva forces have for long been shouting loud about Muslim appeasement, and secular forces have been countering this false propaganda through figures of employment, ownership of corporate houses, educational data, etc., all of which point towards the backwardness of Muslims in relation to Hindu and also other religious minorities. Nevertheless, there has been no systematic study of religion as a factor in economy, in the way that there have been studies on the caste/class factor and the need for positive discrimination in the case of dalits.

A recent book by Barbara Harris-White (*India Working: Essays on Society and Economy*, 2003) contains a detailed chapter on just this aspect. Although the figures concerning ownership of corporate houses, access to education, and employment data are similar to what secular activities have been familiar with, there having been hardly any new data provided through government sources. She goes into newer territories, sometimes based on other studies on Muslims in different parts of the country, to argue that religious codes and beliefs have impinged on economy and in many ways determined differential accumulation of economic assets among religious communities and affected employment patterns. In terms of population, even if one discounts the scheduled castes and tribes, which in any case cannot be seen as Hindus despite all claims by the Sangh Parivar, minorities constituted 17 per cent of the population of India in 1999. Therefore, the matter is not one without some significance.

This is, of course, not the main theme of Barbara's book, which as the name signifies is about how India works. Her emphasis is on the intermediate economy and the small town India, which exists and functions as an economy within the framework of corporate capitalism concentrated in metropolitan India where just 12 per cent of the Indian people live. This is where religious and caste networks and patronage/ inequality patterns have a great determining role.

REINFORCING RELIGIOUS INEQUALITIES

A straightforward point that derives from Barbara's argument is that the domain in which obstructive religious ideas prevailed has not been reduced through the way economy has been managed in post-independence India. Religion has not received the push back into the 'private sphere', and in fact she shows that state policies have in fact reinforced religious inequalities, or to use her phrase, 'religious pluralism', in terms of asset distribution and creation among different religious communities. The role of market and the path of planned development followed have been similar. Primarily all this is because of the manner in which religion is treated in the Constitution itself, and because of the manner in which secularism has been defined and taken to be equal accommodation and competitive patronage of social groups and cultural communities, including increasingly in terms of religious communities.

Barbara states, 'Paradoxically, it is because of—not despite—the secularist ambitions of the Constitutions of that distributive politics are organized in part around religions.' It has meant essentially the acceptance of inequality between religions and contestation of idea of equal citizenship itself in class, caste, and religious terms. A failure to desacralize the economy has also meant that competition, particularly in the intermediate economy in small towns, takes the form of rivalries that easily erupt into communal conflicts, as studies of anti-minority programs would show.

UNEQUAL ECONOMIC POWER

A second major point is the nature of unequal economic power. Although minorities constituted 17 per cent of the Indian population, the non-Parsi and non-Jain component, which forms the major chunk of this minority population, controlled only 2 per cent of the assets of the top business houses in 1996, while the Jains and Parsis controlled as much as 40 per cent. The economic significance of the Jains is of course much greater than their share in population.

Besides, although Muslims are twice as urbanized as their population, the share would suggest that (12.6 per cent), mostly Muslims live in rural areas. Figures below the poverty line show the same preponderance for Muslims. Although, disproportionately urban, they are under-represented in the country's capitalist elite. Muslim illiteracy rate is 15 per cent higher for Muslims in relation to Hindus, and the proportion of Hindus who get secondary education is three times that of Muslims. They also have smaller percentage among those self-employed. The incidence of landlessness is much higher among them. The Muslims are disadvantaged in India in many areas of the society.

Among Christians, there is a great difference in the position of Syrian Christians who have been Christians for a long time and who have benefited from educational and employment opportunities during the British rule, retaining their status until today. In addition, Dalits who are recent or nineteenth-century converts from the lower castes and who constitute the agricultural sector, like their Hindu counterparts, are likely to be among those below the poverty line. There is a similar disjunction within the lower caste Sikhs and the land-owning Sikh Jat families, although there is another difference based on religion in Punjab, with Sikhs constituting the peasantry and the Hindus the trading/ shopkeeper castes. Production and exchange neatly compartmentalize on religious lines and caste lines. In addition, while the Sikhs form the major rural population in the Punjab, the Hindus are concentrated in urban areas.

ECONOMIC IMPLICATION OF RELIGIOUS INEQUALITY IN INDIA

Barbara White points out that religious inequality has some correlation with occupational status and class formation in much the same way as caste does, and has been a factor in much of the communal violence as well when it becomes an incidence of protecting or taking over access to assets and surplus. Religious networks easily assume economic organizational forms when these organizations pose as a charity or social welfare organizations. The Hindutva organizations receiving huge funds come to mind as do their role in calling for and successfully implementing economic boycott of the Muslims in Gujarat after first destroying their economic capabilities. It is also considered that personal laws of all religious communities in regulating and determining rights to property, inheritance, etc. also create imbalance in terms of appropriation of surplus and access to economic assets earned or owned by families in terms of gender. When religious inequality as well as caste and gender cease to impinge on economy, we can then say that capitalism has shorn off its feudal remnants. To fight against all these is also to fight for equal citizenship and for the creation of class solidarities among working people, which are also the best guarantors for democracy in India, and the rest of the world since the principle of egalitarian needs to be universal.

RELIGIOUS INEQUALITY AS A PLAYER IN TENSION AND CONFLICT

Religion with its attached inequality may generate tension as well as conflict, but they may also help towards their resolution. It may justify, motivate inequality, or even mandate war and violence, but they also require tolerance, peace, and global co-existence. Sometimes religious groups attack each other, religious leaders issue bellicose statements that are very incompatible with the teachings and values of their own traditions. The dilemma here is whether religion's place in the public realm should be minimized because its manipulation fuels tension and conflicts, or even strengthens it.

I know how much Pope John Paul II tried through the call for peace talks among different religious denominations to bridge the gap and reduce conflict among religions. He brought together in 1992 all leaders of different religions in order to limit misunderstanding and contempt one faith holds against the other and to impress on them the idea of inter dialogue. In addition, after the 11 September terrorist attack in the United States, he called for another peace talk initiative for all religious leaders, which helped to defuse the tension between Islam and the West.

In terms of internal tension and conflict, it is extremely difficult to separate specifically religious inequality, motivation, and factors from the political, cultural, and ethnic elements behind the strife. Most studies suggest that cases in which religion is the principal misuse of violent conflict are extremely rare; some say that the basis is far more commonly economic, political, and ideological in nature. However, politicians hide behind religion as a means to reach their political goals, not minding the tension it creates. David Little of the United States Institute of Peace identifies three contemporary internal conflicts in which religious factors with its inequality are central: Sri Lanka (Sinhalese Buddhist vs. Tamil Hindu), Sudan (Muslim vs. Christian), and Ukraine (Russian Orthodox vs. Independence Orthodox vs. Roman Catholic). During the tension, which later culminated into the conflict in Bosnia, leaders of the Islamic, Roman Catholic, and Serbian Orthodox communities there declared, 'The characterization of this tragic conflict as a religious war and the misuse of all religious symbols used with the aim to further hatred, must be proscribed and is condemned.' Nevertheless, the religious dimension of violent conflicts downplayed the apartheid regime in South Africa and the forces promoting ethnic cleansing in the former Yugoslavia certainly manipulated believers, appropriated religious resources, and falsified religious messages for their own ends. Furthermore, most contemporary tension or violent intra-state conflicts do reflect a religious dimension—the conflicts involving the Hindus and Muslims in India, the clashes between different branches of Islam in Iraq or Syria, the tension between Christians and Muslims in Northern Nigeria. Religious issues also justify or fuel many intra-state conflicts such as those between Pakistan and India over Kashmir, between Iran and Iraq, between Israel and Arab or Muslim believers.

The idea of one religion being dominant against the other creates inequality and thereby breeds resentment, tension, and conflict. For instance, in the Middle East, which has been dominated by Sunni government, many Shiite Muslims believed that they are unequally treated and as such feel the impact of inequality. When Iranian Revolution occurred in 1979, the Shiites in Iran took over power, and since then they have been supporting and building up Shiites in other states in the region.

This has created religious tension and conflict around the region and elsewhere. In Lebanon, the Shiite Hezbollah has always clashed with other religions in that nation. Also in Pakistan, there has been suicide attacks carried out by both the Sunnis and Shits against each other. If everyone gets a fair share in the state resources irrespective of his belief, tribe, and ethnic configuration, then the possibility of limiting tension and conflict will not elude us.

The so-called Islamic Jihadist have unequal mentality, in which they have killed their fellow citizens of the same tribe only because of another religion, which is not Islam. When they kill the infidel, which is unequal idea that if you are not Islamic you are of less value than they are and therefore you deserve to die. In places like England and United States, political power has resided unequally in the hands of the Protestants for centuries, thus so the distribution of power designed by Christians of particular religion to dominate others in every area of political climate. The conflict in Northern Ireland that has lasted for decades was also because of religious inequality practiced by the Protestants. The Catholic setting of the Celtics were harmonic before the coming of the Protestants, who hijacked the political power and reduced the Catholics to second-class citizens, thereby perpetuating inequality in the political equation. The history of the Separatist also reveals what religious inequality can do to a society. Until today, the effects of the separatist/acclaimed God's elect where there may be other faiths, are the devil's elect, if I may suggest, has created inequality in American history. But it is also important to note that religious inequality effects on creating tension and violent conflicts are limited in many cases. In the midst of extreme nationalism and ethnic cleansing, one's survival might depend on whether you are Muslim, Orthodox, Hindu, Jewish, or Christian.

Conflicts tend to alter the roles that religious beliefs, practices, and institutions play in society. In such situations, religious traditions reinterpret and manipulate their justifications for the use of arms, such as in Jihad in Islam or 'just war' in the Christian tradition. At the same time, religions redefine themselves in a world of rapid change and increasing tension due to inequality, thereby taking up or rejecting the values of an emerging global culture. However, cases abound where religions have helped to reduce inequality, tension, and conflict when the believers recognize and take into account the importance of religious creed, of love, peace, equality, and justice for all. Such has been the attitude of Pope John Paul II, Martin Luther, and Mother Teresa, who looked beyond a particular religion to heal the divide among people of different faith or religion.

The idea of religious inequality has always played a part in the way some states design government policy, which at times favours a particular religion against another and sometimes encourages separatism among religions. Many around the world believe that Indian government policy favours Hindus than any other religious groups. In Northern Ireland, Protestants and Catholics live separately because they feel safer that way or they have little choice because of the interface created to reduce tension due to religious inequality between the two faiths. Interface is a boundary line between predominantly Protestant area and a predominantly Catholic area of housing. In this interface, inequality still exists among them based on class differences. How can two people reading the same word of Christ Jesus not apply love and harmony to overcome inequality? For we all are equal before the eyes of Jehovah, since Christ Jesus died for all humankind, not for Protestants or Catholics alone. (Mathew 22:37–39, John 3:16) Apostle Paul emphasized the importance of unity among the people of God, for Christ Jesus is not divided. The idea of division brings inequality and inequality breeds tension and conflicts, as it had been the case in Northern Ireland for decades, and will continue to be until people come to recognize that we would not treat people differently and want them to treat us otherwise. 'For the measure we give we will receive', so give love and receive love. The Scripture said that there is no law against equality, fairness, love, justice, and peace. I Corinthians 1:12–13, Romans 12,

Galatians 5:22–26. Let us love as Christ loved us so that we will be able to dwell in peace with one another.

Religion should not be used to aid and support inequality; rather it should serve as an agent for the future of humankind. It is of considerable importance in introducing civilization, perspective and process of social integration, and therefore it should not serve as a means to break the society down. In some cases, religion has become a unifying force for peacemaking such as in South Africa's Post-apartheid Era, and at the same time strengthening possibilities for conflict transformation. Let us use religion to build an integrated society than a divided one based on inequality. Let us hold on to what unites us rather than on what divides us to build a better and fair society, where each one might have equal opportunity to participate and contribute their quota in healing the world that is infected with the disease of inequality.

CHAPTER 6

Inequality Between the Poor and the Rich

There exists an inequality between the rich and the poor as well as in other areas of human society. Poverty has stricken many around the world as a plague that has no cure, and many have become excessively rich than any other in the history of mankind. Since the Industrial Revolution, we have achieved great advancement in science, technology, economics, and democratic institution as well, but all these achievements have improved life for many while greater percentage has become victims of this achievement through unequal treatment.

WHAT IS POVERTY?

It is a state of being poor, lack of the means of providing material needs or comforts, deficiency in finance, scantiness, 'the poverty of feelings that reduced her soul' (Scott Turow). Poverty also means unproductiveness, infertility, the poverty of the soil, having income and wealth too low to maintain a life and health at subsistence. The rich are those who have income enough to maintain and provide for their needs and have surplus to save. The unequal distribution of wealth and income, be it internal or external, has always created unequal status where some will become limited in resources while others have more than abundance. The imbalance between the rich and the poor is a fatal and general illness of all republics.

The difference between the rich and the poor affects many areas of human development and social issues, be it education, health, religious belief, housing, and environment. Education, being one of the means to escape poverty in many cases, becomes difficult to obtain when families are faced with limited resources. Many children around the world are not educated, not because they do not like education but because their parents are so poor that they cannot afford to pay for the school fees. This is the case in most of the Third World or developing countries, as many now call it—from Nigeria to India, Malawi to Pakistan, Yemen to Peru. But in the case of Nigeria, it is a shame that in a country that is the sixth largest producer of oil in the world, many children are unable to even attend primary school which is a fundamental human right. President George W. Bush in his January 2007 address cited education as important in changing the dynamics. He cited that education's role in income inequality 'is real, it has been rising for more than 25 years.' He said the reason is clear: we have an economy that increasingly rewards education, but a situation where some cannot afford to go to school. How can they benefit from the rewards of education?

Many scholars around the globe have seen poverty as a human right issue that needs to be addressed to inject dignity into the life of the poor. The poor's dignity is affected in terms of human rights abuse since the rights to food, housing, and good environment embodied in the human rights article are not made accessible. If people's opportunity or right to food and quality life are limited by the influence of others, possibly the rich, then the fundamental rights of the poor has been violated.

Noble Peace laureate Shirin Ebadi of Iran said, 'any violation of the rights to housing or to health care, education, or food is a human rights violation. Using the resources within the nation or country is a human right. The poor who live in countries that have dictatorship are at an extreme disadvantage because these resources used to enhance the conditions of elite groups. In such societies, people are often born into debt. Women and children are the first victims of extreme poverty. They also face discrimination in law and in practice in many countries in the world. Fighting poverty and the law work together. We also need the tools and mechanism necessary to implement laws effectively because without the correct systems in place, many laws fail to be in place. (Commission on Legal Empowerment of the Poor)

POVERTY AND INEQUALITY IN A GLOBAL SCALE

According to University of California–Berkeley economist J. Bradford De Long (2004), capitalism is hundreds of years old and today dominates nearly every part of the globe. Its champions claim it is the greatest engine of production growth the world has ever seen. He also argued that it is unique in its ability to raise the standard of living of every person on earth. Because of capitalism we are 'slouching towards Utopia', the phrase coined by de Long. Slowly but surely heading towards a world in which everyone will have achieved a United States style of middle class life.

The United States is often referred to as a nation dominated by middle class, and one in which it is relatively easy for the poor person to become a person of means. Here, it said, equality of opportunity rules. It is hard to know what middle class and equality of opportunity mean, but it is fair to think that such a society ought not be one in which people do indeed have a great deal of economic mobility. The data on poverty and inequality of income and wealth do not square very well with this image. In the United States, the Federal Government had defined a poverty level of income as 'one below which families would find it difficult to live without serious problems, which would place them in real danger when faced with any sort of economic crisis, such as a sick child or an injury at work.' This official poverty level of income is equal to three times the minimum food budget calculated by the Department of Agriculture. A very modest standard with numerous restrictive and unrealistic assumptions, for example, those poor families will be able to buy food at the lowest unit price and will know how to convert the cheapest food into nutritious meals.

In 2001, this was $18.32 for a family of four, or $12 for 1 per cent of the population. The incident of poverty was 24 per cent for blacks and 21.8 per cent for Hispanics. In 2002, 35.2 per cent of black children fewer than six years lived in poverty, as did 29.1 per cent Hispanic children.

In the United States in 2002, income inequality was greater than at any time since 1920s with the richest 5 per cent of all households receiving six times more income than the poorest 20 per cent of households, up from about four times in 1970. According to Paul Krugman of the *New York Times*, perhaps as much as 70 per cent of all the income growth in the United States during the1980s went to the richest 1 per cent of all the families. With respect to wealth, in the United States in 1995 the richest 1 per cent of all households owned 42.2 per cent of all stocks, 55.5 per cent of all bonds, 44.2 per cent of all trusts, 71.4 per cent of all noncorporate businesses, and 36.9 per cent of all nonhome real estate. As with income inequality, this has been increasing at least for the past twenty years.

From all these inferences, we can see how the rich continue to get richer and the poor continue to be poorer. The opportunity needed to create wealth has remained in the hands of the rich without any chance for the poor to break through, unless in the case of exceptional lucky poor emerging from their poverty to rise to the top. In most cases, this is 1 out of 1000 poor may be fortunate to have this success.

GAP WIDENING BETWEEN THE RICH AND POOR DESPITE BOOM

In Canada for example, it has become obvious that the rich are getting richer while the income of the poor people continue to stagnate in a time when the wage gap should be shrinking, a new report on the Canadian economy said. Inequality is continuing to grow year after year in spite of the current economic boom—a period of prosperity that would traditionally see the extremes between the wealthy and the poor drawing closer together, the Canadian Centre for Policy Alternative said in a study.

The Ottawa-based independent research institute's report ('The Rich and the Rest of Us'), says it has been thirty years since the wealthy and the poor were so far divided in how much they earn. What's more, the share of overall income going to 80 per cent of Canadian families is less than it was a generation ago. Last fall, CCPA released a poll suggesting three quarters of Canadians believe inequality is growing. Still, there is hope the study notes. Nearly half of Canadians who are raising children have not experienced a free fall in their incomes, thanks largely to the government tax and transfer system and especially the tax-free monthly Canada's child tax benefit, says the study. Even the prime minister of Canada Pierre Trudeau confirmed the presence of inequality in Canada. He said never before in history has the disparity between the rich and the poor, the comfortable and the starving, been so extreme.

Britain in the issue of inequality between the rich and the poor or economic divide in British society is not left out, if I may say. The wealth gap in British society has reached its highest level for more than forty years, says one report in 2007, creating clusters of rich and poor who destined never to be exposed to one another. The report carried out by Joseph Rowtree Foundation found that 'average' families had virtually disappeared in some areas, while, however in some societies, some people have remained poor because they fail to take the chance offered to them. However, a majority are poor because of the system designed to keep some in poverty. During the slavery days in the United States, blacks were not allowed to own their own businesses even when they have the skill to do so. They are not allowed to buy houses which also helps to create wealth for generations to come, and this type of system is somehow still in existence in institutionalized racism.

Wealthy households in Britain were increasingly concentrated in the outskirts of major cities. Although the labour party promises to heal the divide between the rich and the poor, somehow it has failed to deliver. According to ONS that provide statistics information and figures, the gap between the rich and the poor have continued to increase since 2004–2005 and until to date, 16 per cent of the population in Great

Britain live in low-income households and the figures have increased to 20 per cent in recent years.

Aristotle said that some lose, some expand their original homesteads, and suddenly we have hoi beltistoi and hoi polloi, and the rallying cry that someone's liberty to do as he pleases means that egalitarianism of the lowest common denominator becomes impossible. According to Victor Davis Hanson, he has seen communities and families in which equal inheritances soon led to radically different outcomes as siblings on rocky ground thrives, while another in deep loam starves. One town with abundant resources goes broke, while another without natural advantage thrives. One example is in the case of Japan and India, Nigeria and the Netherlands. Japan is a country without many natural resources but succeeded in becoming rich, whereas India has many natural resources but has remained poor over the years.

Another example is the Netherlands vs. Nigeria, a country with a lot of natural resources but has remained poor and will continue to be poor, not as a curse but as a result of bad management and bad governance. Her citizens have remained in abject poverty, while The Netherlands is not endowed with natural resources but is rich and succeeded in providing for its citizenry. The poverty level between these two countries cannot compare in any way.

However, we all know that there is no way the society can be 100 per cent equal, but we are talking of reducing the great gap of inequality among nations as well as between citizens of the same state. Look at the situation where only 1,100 people in the world of 6.5 billion people own the world's wealth; a global society wherein in the United States alone, people spend $42 billion dollars yearly on pets—dogs, cats, birds, etc., when some cannot even afford health care, which is a human right issue. Some poverty is created, just as in a situation wherein a qualified immigrant doctor or engineer can only drive a cab in Canada, or a qualified immigrant in the Netherlands is locked up for six to twelve years in asylum procedure without no hope of future. Their dignity stolen or has been reduced to the barest minimum. Automatically, these people are barely going to remain poor because their future and progress are mortgaged or limited by the arms of the state policy. In a situation like this inequality becomes obvious in the eyes of those who know what is inequality, but to those who appreciate it, it sounds right to them.

Remember the Bible in the book of Deuteronomy, it says, 'When you beat your olive trees, you shall not go over the boughs again, it shall be for the sojourner's, the fatherless and widows.' Today, how many Christians care about this, instead they steal from the poor and never allow them access to the boughs after harvest. 'Do not rob the poor because he is poor, or crush the afflicted at the gate.' This has become the passion of the rich to rob the poor and crush the afflicted as hard as they can.

THE POOR AND THE RICH IN MANHATTAN

In Manhattan, poor people make two cents for each dollar to the rich. Sam Roberts said, 'The Trump Tower on Fifth Avenue is only about sixty blocks from the Wagner House in East Harlem, but they might as well be lightyears apart.' This epitomizes the highest- and lowest-earning census tracts in Manhattan, where the disparity between the rich and poor is now greater than in any other county in the United States. That finding, in an analysis conducted for *The New York Times*, dovetails with other new regional economic research, which identifies the Bronx as the poorest urban county in the US, and suggests that the middle class in New York State is depleted.

The fifth earners in Manhattan now make fifty-two times what the lowest fifth make: $365,826 compared with $7,047, which is roughly compared to the income disparity in Namibia, according to the *Times* analysis of 2000 census data. Put another way, for every dollar made by households in the top fifth of Manhattan earners, households in the bottom fifth made about 2 cents. That represents a substantial widening of the income gap from previous years. In 1980, the top fifth of earners made twenty-one times what the bottom fifth made in Manhattan, which ranked seventeenth among the nation's income disparity. By 1990, Manhattan ranked second behind Kalawao county, Hawaii, a former leper colony with which it had little in common except for that signature of grove of palm trees at the World Financial Center. The rich in Manhattan made thirty-two times the average of the poor then, or $4,174.49 vs. $5.44. Dr Andrew A. Beveridge, a sociology professor at Queens College of the University of New York, conducted the analysis for the *Times*. The growing disparity in Manhattan helped drive New York from eleventh among cities with biggest disparity (1980), to fifth in 1990 and fourth in 2000, behind Atlanta, Berkeley, California, and Washington. 'The grains are all going to the top,' Dr Beveridge said, 'It is a massive class disparity.' Last time the census bureau reported that even as the economy grew around the nation, incomes stagnate and poverty rates rose.

The Bronx, which has a poverty rate of 30.6 per cent, ranked out only by three border counties in Texas, where living costs are lower. Swollen in part by the earnings of commuters who work in New York City, median household income among the states was highest in New Jersey ($61.359), and Connecticut ($60.528); it was $47.349 in New York State, also above the national median. Edward Wolff a New York University economist attributed the growing disparity to ballooning Wall Street incomes and declining wages for lower skilled workers. Though these forces are at work across the country, he said, 'the heavy preponderance of corporate headquarters, the financial sector, and the legal sector in New York City have made the increase in the ratio of income between the top and quintile more extreme than in other parts of the country.' The elites, the top silver of the income scale, can drive consumprion and investment forward while the bottom half slogs along. Wolff said, 'If inequality had embedded within its own seeds of destruction, it would implode sooner than later, but that doesn't appear to be the case. Many who have fallen from behind have skewed notion of their prospects for the upward mobility.' Jared Bernstein, senior economists at the Liberal Economic Policy Institute, said that the income gap which is in Manhattan has historically been large and can endure indefinitely.

HUMAN RIGHTS AND EXTREME POVERTY

Report of the United Nations Commission on Human Rights 1993

The Universal Declaration of Human Rights proclaims that everyone is entitled to a standard of living adequate to provide for health and well-being of oneself and one's family. Moreover, in accordance with the Universal Declaration of Human Rights International, covenants recognize that freedom from fear and want can be achieved only if everyone enjoys economic, social, and cultural rights in addition to civil and political rights. In this light, the Baha'i International Conference offered few thoughts about human rights and extreme poverty.

The increasing disparity between the rich and the poor is a major destabilizing influence in the world. It produces and exacerbates regional and national tension, conflict, environmental degradation, crime, violence, and illicit drug use. These consequences of extreme poverty affect all individuals and nations. Increasingly, we are becoming aware that we are all members of a single human family. In the family, the suffering of any member is felt by all, and until that suffering is alleviated, no member of the family can be fully happy or at ease. Few are able to look at starvation and extreme poverty without feeling a sense of failure.

Baha'i approach to the problem of extreme poverty is based on the belief that economic problems are solved only through the application of spiritual principles. This approach suggests that to adjust the economic relationships of society, man's character must transform first. I remember that Pope John Paul II said, 'Free trade is not enough to regulate markets. Free trade can work quite well between equal partners. Free trade between unequal states can be disastrous. Therefore, until the actions of humankind promote justice above the satisfaction of greed, and readjust the world's economies accordingly the gap between the rich and the poor will continue to widen. The dream of sustainable economic growth, peace, and prosperity must remain elusive. Sensitizing mankind to the vital role of spirituality in solving economic problems, including the realization of universal equitable access to wealth and opportunity will we are convinced create a new impetus for change.'

VIOLATION OF THE RIGHTS OF THE POOR

The poor have always been the victims of the rich, be it rich nations against poor nations or rich people against poor people. We always hear that the law is no respecter of anybody, but that is in theory not in practice. The rights of people are violated because they are poor, and the poor cannot afford quality lawyers to defend their rights and uphold justice in their favour. The rich have always and will continue to take advantage of the poor either by fair or foul means, no matter how loud we shout, but we only demand for a society where the poor is treated with compassion and fairness with respect to human rights provision, which all nations endorsed.

Global climate today is characterized by two contradictory phenomena: increased insecurity that occurred after the 11 September 2001 terrorist attack in New York, and the confluence and solidarity of global civil society responding to the serious impact of economic globalization on the world's poor. The first creates uncertainty in the world and the second creates hope. It is good to use the transition period to reaffirm universally accepted principles of human rights, which will guide our short- and long-term actions to understand the root causes of tension, conflict, and terrorism. The UN for over fifty years has achieved a lot in the direction of human rights and dignity of man, in the fight against discrimination, for self-determination, non-retrogression, gender equality, etc. The principles of the UN give direction to states, nations, local and international government responsibility. Under the United Nations Charter (Articles 55 and 56) in the Universal Declaration of Human Rights Article 28, these state that nations and international government are given the mandate to take action on the rights for food, housing, work, education, on tackling issues of wealth and land redistribution. Irrespective of these declarations, many poor people's rights to all these are violated daily by those in authority, since the poor has no right to question them, but we have to remember that one day the silence of the poor will be broken and violence will ensue.

Globalization must be within the primacy of human rights protection. There must be a policy for poverty reduction by both national and international states. The human rights of nondiscrimination are the core value of human rights, be it racial, religious, economic, social, or cultural. In the current global climate of income disparity and the gap between the rich and the poor, it is important to note that discrimination and segregation in economic, social, and cultural rights are based not only on race, class, or gender, but can also result from poverty and economic marginalization. 'Non-discrimination and equality are integrated in the elements of the international human rights normative framework, including the International Covenant on Economic, Social and Cultural Rights (ICESCR). Sometimes poverty arises when people have no access to existing resources because of who they are, what they believe in, or where they live.

Discrimination can cause poverty, just as poverty can cause discrimination. Inequality may be entrenched in institutions and deeply rooted in social values that shape relationships within households and communities. Accordingly, the international norms of nondiscrimination and equality, which demand that particular attention, given to the vulnerable groups and individuals from such groups have profound implications for anti-poverty strategies.

Institutionalized discrimination found patterns of violation of economic, social and cultural rights, so it is important that states make the effort as well as for civil society to be watchful. However, since the Durban Conference held in 2001, much has changed in terms of implementation of the declaration and program of action that emerged from it. We owe the poor nothing less than the full human rights that the pursuit of their dignity deserves and our action judged by nothing than whether we are able to achieve the inevitable task for them. Global economic integration will contribute to the improvement of living standard and reduction of inequity and inequality if it is down sincerely without the same attitude of inequality and discrimination against others. We should also remember that dignity is inherent in every person simply because of his or her being human. It is being and not having. 'It does not come from status, nationality, ethnicity, or any human accomplishment; it belongs to being and should be limited to something people have.' So let us allow the poor the dignity by allowing them to have access to education, food, housing, and social values.

The justice system around the globe has shown how the rights of the poor are violated every day by states and their institutions. Max Weber, a prominent sociologist has affirmed that race, ethnicity, and poverty do play an important role in sentencing the United States, as well as many countries around the world. Offenders, from minorities, young, male, and unemployed are more likely to go to prison. The rich can afford to buy justice while the poor are doomed despite justice being on their side. When the bushmen of Botswana were dispossessed of their land for industrial development, they were just thrown out of their land without any consideration, but if they were the rich elites, no one would have even dared to do it, instead heaven be let loose. The same happened in Nigeria in the late 1980s, when the poor living at Muoruko Lagos were displaced from their slums, the government and political class took the land and redistributed it among themselves. None of poor people were redressed in the judiciary system that was manned by corrupt officials.

THE POOR, HEALTH, AND EDUCATION

Life expectancy is a measure of one's health and is commonly used to gauge the quality of life of the people. The rich are able to pay for good and quality health care, thus, they have better health care; whereas the poor can only settle for what is available to them. Eating well and living an active life is more possible for the rich than for the poor who cannot afford to cover the cost of quality life. Today in the United States, 42 million people are without health insurance and these are the poor that cannot afford the high cost of health insurance. Yet still, the rich are opposed to health care reforms that will give others a better chance to have one.

When the poor around the world become sick with chronic disease, only God can save them, but if it happens to the rich, they will survive because they can afford to pay to live on. The shopping of human parts has proved how far the rich can go to live at the expense of the poor. The shopping of human parts for transplant from the poor to the rich has become the highest market in India and Pakistan. China is one of the fastest growing economy in the world that has the darkest part of it to human parts market. The poor sell their kidney, lungs, liver at a price that is worth nothing but $1000, while the middle men rips a whooping amount of $20,000–50,000 dollars paid by the rich in Europe and the United States who continue to live while many poor are dying for giving out their organs.

There was a case in India, where a father sold his kidney for a price of chicken only to be faced with his own child needing the kidney for survival. He has sold one of his for a small amount, but cannot provide for his child or be able to buy one to keep him alive. This is a new trend where the poor is robbed to save the rich. Please let us be humane for one minute and think about the life of those that God created as he created us.

In the area of education, poverty has limited and restricted many around the globe from having access to at least basic education. In a society today that is based more and more on one's credentials, it is no doubt that the gap between the haves and have-nots is still present in our modern society. In spite of the universal education system instituted in most of the modern nations, there remains a large inequality in the education students receive which is largely based on economics. The rich will go to the best schools while the poor can manage what is available as education. I remember a child in primary school when the world and UN were talking and launched The International Year of the Child. They talked about when all children around the world will have equal access to education. Now I am an adult and it has not happened. Education can do a lot in people's lives—transform their mindset, philosophy, health, improve management of tension, conflict, racism, and other social vices facing the global society. It creates liberal thinking and understanding of crisis and conflict management. Education makes it easier for people to improve their health condition, by having better understanding how health is related to maintaining and having clean environment, thereby reducing the abuse of their environs, which in turn damages their health. Those who are poor tend to live in polluted areas as in slums, as you see Venezuela, Mumbai India, Lagos Nigeria, Soweto South Africa. The poor are always victims of many damn things because of the excruciating poverty.

Presently, the corrupt government officials and political elites in Nigeria are sending their children outside the country to study at the expense of the poor. Those who are supposed to reform social issues for the benefit of the masses do not care about the people. The Nigerian educational system is in a complete mess. The children of the poor bears the brunt of their inefficiency, while the children of the rich has the option to go to Ghana or abroad to get a better education.

However, I blame the Nigerian civil society or the masses that has refused to revolt and rise up against the political class that is mortgaging their future and that of their children.

ERADICATION OF POVERTY

Poverty is an infectious disease, which can transfer from generation to generation, You may not agree with me but I have seen it happen. Many families, nations, and states have remained poor for over six decades without any sign of coming out of it. It has ravaged societies around the globe. It has helped in creating a lot vices we are facing today in a global scale, which no one could have anticipated. A curse needs to be broken. It affects every facet of human society and therefore needs to be tackled squarely.

Poverty eradication is one of the eight Millennium Development Goals of the United Nations, which it wants to achieve by 2015, but unfortunately, it is increasing with the recent system of globalization and the economic crises. The world has made significant progress in reducing poverty as one of its agenda.

Between 1990 and 2002, the average overall incomes increased by approximately by 21 per cent according to UN report of the Millennium Development Goals. The people in extreme poverty declined by an estimated 130 million. Child mortality rates fell from 103 deaths per 1,000 live births a year to 88. Life expectancy rose from 63 years to nearly 65 years. An additional 8 per cent of the developing world's people received access to water. An additional 15 per cent has acquired access to improved sanitation services.

However, to me as a Nigerian from Africa, when I take stock of how many have died in my little village in a month, I begin to doubt if countries in Africa such as mine is included in this study by the UN. At least when you watch Western televisions and the image created of African people and their countries, you can see as well and have the same doubt as me concerning the improved lives and services reported by the UN's MDGs.

Nevertheless, progress has been far across countries. There are huge disparities across and within countries. There is a huge urban poverty that is also extensive, growing, and underreported by traditional indicators.

Sub-Sahara Africa is an epicenter of crisis, with continual food insecurity, a rise of extreme poverty, stunning high child and maternal mortality, and large numbers of people living in slums—widespread shortfalls for most of the Millennium Development Goals. Asia is the region with the fastest progress, but even so, there are hundreds of millions of their people who remain in extreme poverty. And even fast-growing countries fail to achieve some of the non-income goals. Other regions have mixed records, notably Latin America, the transition economies, and Middle East and North Africa, often with slow or no progress on some of the MDG and persistent inequalities undermining progress on others. A promise to the world that a better future is possible for everyone. The Millennium Goals will empower millions of people with the opportunity to learn, grow and break out of poverty. Each time one person escapes poverty, it creates hope for others to think that a better day is possible. But if we continue to press down the poor without allowing them access to develop themselves and emerge from poverty, the ugly nature of poverty and its effects will continue to ravage our society. Governments and institutions such as the UN, and others should do more in alleviating poverty for real instead of the rhetoric we have been hearing over three decades.

Without reducing poverty, its root causes such as inequality, tension, crime, and violent conflict will never end. Remember, a hungry man is an angry man, says Bob Marley in his music.

CHAPTER 7

Tension and Conflict as a Result of Inequality and Some Solutions

It is a well-known and established fact that inequality and unequal treatment meted out against people around the world is the major source of violence, tension, armed struggle, and conflict. Anna Tibaijuka, United Nations Habitat executive director warned in 2004, before the release of the The State of The World Cities how 'extremism is likely to flourish in the world's rapidly spreading slums if government does not tackle the poverty that fuels it'. In 2030, an estimated five billion people will be urban dwellers, of which two billion will be slum dwellers. With the recent economic crisis today, this number of slum people around the globe might exceed the projected 2030 slum dwellers. At least recently, the number of people that are homeless has increased with people losing their homes since they cannot afford to pay any more. Slums, according to the UN definition, are rundown areas of the city characterized by substandard housing and squalor and lacking in tenure security. According to the UN, the proportions of urban dwellers living in slums decreased from 47 per cent to 37 per cent in developing world between 1990 and 2005. However, due to the rising population, the number of slum dwellers has increased. For instance, Kibera in Kenya the second largest in Africa, and third largest in the world, Libertador in Venezuela, Ciudad Perdidad in Mexico, Agege in Lagos Nigeria, Tai Hong in Hong

Kong, Eilshoppgate, a former slum in Wetherby, West Yorkshire, UK. It is said that two out of every three urban dwellers live in slums.

As a global society that wants to improve, government and institutions have to take initiatives that will alleviate poverty, housing conditions as well as increasing opportunities that will create room for people to emerge from poverty, so that they can improve their standard of living. It is obvious that crime and violence are dominant in the slums; as people's lives change their mentality also changes. The more slum dwellers are able to get better life through opportunities in education and jobs, they can abandon violence, crime, and will not be target for those who create conflict. For example, in Nigeria, the people of Niger Delta are those who are involved in kidnapping and blowing up oil pipelines, and these are slum dwellers. They always offer their services to those who are ready to provide them an escape route from a life of poverty. So then we as a society should be able to design development programs that offer a better and improved living to the poor and slum dwellers, so there will be less conflict and associated tension. Bob Marley said that 'a hungry man is an angry man', so you cannot deter a hungry man from being angry.

In the course of writing this book, it has become obvious to me and some of you who will read this book, that inequality in race, wealth and income, health, poverty, religion, and political power, distribution of land and resources as the causes of tension and conflict around the world. It might be in Sri Lanka, India, Nigeria, Sudan, Rwanda, United States, England, Russia, Netherlands, Canada, Australia, Iraq, Iran, etc. It has been shown that religion with its attached inequality may generate tension and conflict, but may also help towards their resolution. In many cases, it has justified inequality or even mandated war and violence both in the past and present. The crusades and Jihads prove what religious inequality can do in terms of breeding conflict.

The claim of superiority by some religions as being better than the others has fuelled tension and conflict among believers. The Sunni Islam has fought against the Shiite Islam since the death of Prophet Mohammed in 632 CE. The fight of who is the true guardian of Islam has generated unending conflict since then. In most of the

Islamic nations, the Sunnis has dominated the power and the Shiites have felt unequally treated or represented and as result they always resort to violence and conflict both internal and external from Iran to Iraq, Lebanon to Syria, Saudi Arabia to Kuwait, Pakistan to India, Afghanistan, Nigeria, Sudan, Malaysia, etc. This tension and conflict between the Sunnis and the Shiites has spilled over to other people who have nothing to do with it because when there is conflict many are affected whether you are a part of it or not. Part of the global terrorism we are all suffering today stems from a war that lasted over 1,300–1,400 years between the Sunni Muslims and the Shiite. Each sect fears and dreads the other instead of living in harmony and peace with understanding that Allah is one, is not Sunni or Shiite; he is God Almighty.

After the Iranian revolution of 1979, the Shiite-led government in Iran had influence and supported all Shiites communities throughout the Middle East and encouraged them to take control of their governments as it occurs in Lebanon, Bahrain and is also likely to happen in Saudi Arabia. If nothing is done to address the issue, the animosity between the Sunnis and Shiite will continue with political domination of either the Sunnis or upcoming Shiites. The case between the two faiths is the same in Malaysia, Afghanistan, and Pakistan. The Hindu-dominated government in India also sparks confrontation and agitation from the Muslim who believe that they are unequally treated by the Hindu religious society, which dominates the government and other institutions. Also in Sri Lanka, the Tamil Hindus have been fighting against the Sin hales Buddhist that has dominated power without equal representation opportunity for the Tamil. When we look at the unending religious conflict in Northern Nigeria, we see the same pattern of religion playing a part, or in Sudan where the Muslim North has been busy over the years mistreating and killing Christians because of difference in religion. The Sudanese Islamic government has extended her Jihad against the African descendants of Sudan in Darfur since 2003 and the conflict is ongoing.

The Northern Ireland tension and conflict has been raging on since over three decades. The religious ideology expressed by both Protestants and Catholics has created one of the longest religious conflicts in Christendom. The dominant attitude of the Protestants against the Catholics and its associated inequality has made it impossible for the conflict to be resolved. These Christians forgot that God is love and Jesus Christ is the king of peace not war. For his kingdom is righteousness, peace, and joy in the Holy Ghost, so their attachment to doctrines is no more important than Christ himself. So let us leave the things that divide us and dwell on that which unites us.

The world needs to use religion to unite people, rather than using it as a means to divide and rule and support inequality, tension, and conflict. Let us do what Mohandas Gandhi said to the British colonialist: 'We all have to apply the Sermon on the Mount which Jesus Christ preached when he was here on earth.' Matthew 5:1–12. With these in our heart every day, we will be able to solve half of the world's problems. We also need to encourage inter denomination dialogue among different faiths in order to bridge the gap of divide which will usher in a better peaceful future for all of us.

GENDER INEQUALITY AND ASSOCIATED TENSION AND REMEDIES

Inequality of gender has also shown that tension and conflict can emanate from all forms of unequal treatment of others whom we think to be different from us. Female gender has been discriminated against for centuries all around the world, both now and in the past, though in some nations, the situation has improved dramatically. We need to give women a chance to participate on equal footing with men because if not, there is bound to be clash or confrontation and conflict.

When the government of Britain refused to listen to the women suffrage movement in 1905, they created a stir. Christabel Pankhurst and Anne Kenney interrupted political meetings in Manchester. From that moment on, their peaceful attitude turned violent and created more tension and conflict between the women activists and the government. They were beaten, tortured, and imprisoned. The action of the government made these women to become extreme in character to obtain their demand, which eventually led to the death of Emily Wilding Davison, when she threw herself under the king's horse in June 1913. She was killed on the spot. Her death turned the violent chapter in the movement struggle for equality, though her death was a setback for the movement but it also moved government to action to address the issue. Also, we know of the radical movement of women suffragists under Alice Paul in 1917, as well as the Occoquan workplace brutality of the state police against women fighting for equal and better treatment in the United States.

We demand a better and equal opportunity for women so that they can contribute their quarter in reshaping the unequal society we live in today. Women need education as men do because it gives women greater choices to function. Many girls under school age are denied this opportunity thereby limiting them the social and economic benefits for the society. Educated women have more economic opportunities and engage more fully in public life. It improves their, health, parenting and helps them to apply preventive measures over diseases. So let us join hands to create equal chance for women as well as men to avoid tension and conflict for the future. Let the world eliminate sexism and discrimination or in fact reduce the level of sexism that exists between the two sexes.

RACIAL /ETHNIC INEQUALITY – TENSION AND SOLUTIONS

Racial and ethnic discrimination and inequality contravene the 1776 United States Declaration of Independence, the 1778 Declaration of the Rights of Man and Citizens issued during the French Revolution, and also the 1948 Universal Declaration of Human Rights signed after World II, which all postulate equality of all men or human beings.

In 1950, under the suggestion of about twenty-one UNESCO scholars to drop the word 'race' and use 'ethnic groups', the scholars such as Levi Strauss Gunnar, Ashley Montagau, and others condemned the scientific racism theory that has played a role in the Holocaust. Race and ethnicity have been the major cause of tension and conflict in centuries and continue to do so, irrespective of all the declarations and conventions adopted by many government around the world. Time has come when we all have to get real and abandon racism and ethnicity.

The genocide/ethnic cleansing in the Holocaust, slavery, and horrible lynching of one another has been because of these two. People played around race and ethnicity to fuel tension and conflict every day around the world. After the Holocaust, nations, institutions, organizations, and treaties said 'never again'. But it happened again and again—in the 1967 genocide of the Nigerian government against the Ibos of Biafra, where over 3 million Ibos were massacred; in Rwanda in 1994 claiming 800,000 to 1 million; in Turkey vs. ethnic Armenia, 2 million; in Bosnia, Tamils name it but the West stood and watched, and never did a damn thing.

The United States today as the world power and a model of democracy still allow race and ethnicity with its associated inequality to dominate its policy like many other countries around the world. This has generated tension and conflict in the past and still going to generate more conflict if we do not unite and say no to racism and ethnic divide no matter where it exists. It is wrong and it is killing our society. You see it in every corner, even now in the football field and other sports activities that was used in the past to solve the problem of race and ethnic tension. During the Apartheid South Africa regime, race bred one of the worst human tension, violence, and conflict we have seen in the recent century and still exists today. Last time South African blacks went on rampage against their fellow Africans, only because they were not South African indigenes. The violence led to the destruction of life and properties. Today, Russian foreigners, mostly black students in Russia, have become a target of racial killing and attacks, while the Russian government turns a blind eye.

The dirty history of American race tension and conflicts cannot be erased from the history books. Recently, many Nazi-KKK ideologists are busy preparing to start another race war as was in the eighteenth and nineteenth century. Their race/ethnic superiority even claimed their own which is why we have to oppose those mad fellows who need education to learn how to co-habitate with others. The death of people like Robert and John F. Kennedy, Martin Luther King Jr., Emmet Till, and others, is a lesson the racists should learn. The riot that erupted after the assassination of Martin Luther King Jr. claimed a lot of lives, a majority of the victims were whites—possibly the innocent who may not be racists—so this is the adverse effect of ethnoracial inequality and its associated tension.

The conflict between the Hutus and the Tutsis dates back to the blood history which stained the twentieth century, from the slaughter of 80,000 to 200,000 Hutus by the Tutsi army in Burundi in 1992 to the 1994 Rwanda genocide, in which the Hutu militias targeted Tutsis, resulting in the massacre of 800,000 to 1 million people in 100 days. The conflict stemmed from the class warfare with Tutsis, who were perceived to have greater wealth and social status as well as favourite cattle ranching over what is seen as the lower-class farming of the Hutus. The influence of the colonial powers in supporting the minority Tutsi's domination over the majority Hutu group also is a factor that culminated in the divide and inequality that exists between the two.

The Roman Catholic Missionary 'White Fathers' is also guilty of creating a race inequality between the Hutus and the Tutsis when they came to Rwanda in late 1880s. They developed a Hamitic theory of race origin which taught that the Tutsis were a superior race. Religion played a role in forming a racial division between the Hutus and the Tutsis. All these factors prepared the ground for tension and conflict that culminated in the 1994 genocide and continues to boil somehow until the present. Unless the wrongs are made right by creating equality between the two to eliminate the inequality that exists, it is most likely we are bound to witness the same conflict in the future. Those holding the superior power in the society, be it the majority or the minority group, established a system of inequality by dominating the less powerful groups. This system is maintained and perpetuated through the social forces. As the late US president Reagan said to Gorbachev of Russia to 'tear down the wall'. That we have to say to all who dominate the less powerful or whether it is the majority or minority: they should tear down the wall of inequality. All states and nations need to respect all international conventions in which they were a signatory in order to respect and honour the dignity of all men, to avoid protest and violence. Ghasi Das Chamars of North India (1756–1836) founded a sect called Satnami and preached the unity of God and the equality of all human beings. This was a direct challenge and protest against Brahiminic hegemony in the name of religion perpetrated against the untouchables by the Hindus. In 1927, the untouchables burned the Manu Smriti at Mahad, as an expression of anger against unequal treatment of others. We need to seek for a more integrated society, respect for human rights, and the rights of all citizens.

WEALTH/INCOME INEQUALITIES – TENSION AND CONFLICT ASSOCIATED WITH IT AND SOLUTIONS

The issue of race, ethnicity, gender, and other forms of inequalities plays a role in income and wealth inequality in any given society; it is like a transferred aggression that spills over. All forms of inequality and discrimination act as a factor in formulating wealth and income distribution by governments, state, local, and institutions. Those who dominate power tend to create a system of inequality that favours their kind, be it tribe, race, gender, etc. Every man is never happy when he is cheated or humiliated, so we should not be like the Bolsheveiks who hated oppressive power and inequality of all kinds, but in reality, they did oppress the people more than did the tsars of Russia.

The Russian Revolution would not have been possible without the power of the union of workers who were facing inequality in income and wealth distribution. The agitation created an undesirable atmosphere for the government to function as well as tension and conflict that led to the overthrow of the Tsarist regime. In the United States, many scholars have confirmed the widening gap in income and wealth among social classes. The disparities in income and wealth in the United States and around the world may be a new ground to launch a revolution of the poor against the rich. The social movement today against international conferences like in Davos and Cancun, Mexico, demonstrates how violence and conflict is around the corner concerning the issue of wealth and income disparities. It has become an internal as well as global problem.

The report commissioned by the International Trade Union Confederation in 2008 shows clearly that based on their survey of sixty-three countries, there is a significant gender pay gap. Women still earn lower than men do even when they have a high level of education. This is a disturbing trend even in the Western world; women still earn less than men do in many countries around the world. ED Wolff of the United States says that the share of national wealth is owned by the richest 1 per cent and doubled during the past three decades. Also, Andrew Jared Bernstein says that income inequality has skyrocketed nearly as fast; these are startling changes in the relative affluence of the country's population over a very short period of time.

Wealth is that which you can use to reproduce income. In the case where wealth is available to a limited number of people, race, gender, and class, the anger of those who are barred from participating because of lack of income and wealth will endure forever. The silence of the poor and disadvantaged will break one day, then comes the conflict against the rich and wealthy. We should not ignore it because we know how angry people were during the financial crises and over bonuses awarded to the wealthy. The super rich have to be careful, if not the next coming revolution is likely to come to their doorpost. When the houses of the poor are repossessed by banks who failed the people, the people has the right to vent their anger on the banks as what happened in England in the past. Racial and ethnic discrimination and inequality limit certain race to own property, which will enable them to regenerate income or assets for future generation.

Governments—local, state, federal—and international agents need a collective action to address the issue of wealth and income inequality. The policy of discrimination need to be reduced in order to have equal distribution of wealth and reduction of income gap. A program of action is necessary to limit greed and their desire for selfishness where people care only about themselves and immediate families. Globalization and integration have to take into account human rights laws to respect the poor and to open opportunities so that the poor can have jobs and improve their standard of living. Tax cuts by governments should take into consideration the poor, and not continue the system where the rich gets tax cuts to the detriment of the poor or the middle class. There is a need for the government to redistribute income from those with more income to those with less. In the United States, for example the distribution of pre-tax income is highly unequal. Study found that the top 10 per cent of households with average income of about $200,000 received 42 per cent of all pre-tax money income in the late 1990s. The top 1 per cent of households averaging $800,000 of income receives 15 per cent of all the pre-tax money income. There is a sharp fall in inequality around the outbreak of World War II and an extended rule in inequality that began in the mid-1970s, and which accelerated in the 1980s. Income inequality today is about as large as it was in the 1920s.

It is saddening that after the growth the world has seen in the twentieth and twenty-first century, we are still living and witnessing great disparities in income and wealth. Globalization continues to favour the rich and highly industrialized nations of the world while the developing countries continue to thrive in poverty and low standard of living. There is a need for the rich countries to have a program of action to assist the developing countries in free market and access to international labour. Wealth should not be limited to only a particular race, ethnic, class or group of people as it was in the eighteenth and late nineteenth century when women as well as black people were not allowed to own properties or start their own business. All these bottlenecks when eliminated can help people develop themselves in every area of life. The restrictions placed on women in owning properties in both England and United States in 1918 and the African Americans in the late seventeenth and early nineteenth century contributed to the lack of more transferable assets in the African American communities in the United States and women in England and around the world. There is a need for all states and government to meet up their obligations signed in international conventions. The anger of those with little should never be under estimated because one day they will revolt against the super rich.

SOCIAL INEQUALITY—TENSION, CONFLICT, AND SOLUTIONS

We all know that classes are mutually antagonistic; the interests of different classes do not coincide in any way. Conflicts are inevitable and define how society develops. The stratification that occurs in society is always a source of tension and conflict between different classes. Those who are socially marginalized can always create conflict in the society. When we look at the caste system around the world, we see the humiliation people go through because of social inequality created by man against his fellowmen. The oppressed will one day reject the tool of oppression, and when that begins, conflict is inevitable.

When the blacks in America were denied their voting rights, they endured for some time until a day when the people rose up and said, 'enough is enough'. They took to the streets to protest and demand for their social rights to participate in election and democratic process. It created tension and conflict between those who need their social rights and those who are against equality. Social inequality prevents others from equal opportunity to quality education, since the wealthy class tends to create exclusive areas in educational field, so that their siblings will have better education system than siblings of the poor or a particular class. It also prevents certain people from having access to the same housing, health care, etc.

The way people behave socially, whether it is discrimination or racism tends to trickle down on the opportunities wealthy individuals can generate for themselves. A perfect example of this is in Thomas Shapiro's book *The Hidden Cost of Being African American*, he demonstrates how unequal the 'playing field' is for blacks and whites. For instance, middle-class families, one black and the other white, are given different opportunities in the housing market. The black family was denied a loan from the bank for housing, whereas the white family was approved.

This is a noticeable incident considering that home ownership is one of the main ways Americans acquire wealth.

There is a need for the global society to deal with racial, ethnic, and cultural stereotyping of people. We are becoming more and more a global family, and therefore we have to try to work together to eliminate social ills plaguing human society. The voices of liberal enlightenment should shout louder for positive change, application, and enforcement of human rights laws, and respect for human dignity. Tension, violence, and conflict can be avoided if we shun inequalities of all kind and embrace an egalitarian attitude, in which all and sundry will be able to function and participate in every sector of the society. This can limit the poverty created by conflict displacement, lack of security, and food shortages, which are all part of the consequences of conflict. There is a need for global action to reduce the social chasm that is growing between the super rich and the rest of the world population.

Social life and good standard of living should not be limited to the few while the rest of the world suffers. Though it is not possible to have an equal world, we need to do our best to reduce the gap of social inequality. We need to take action to make sure that all rectified human rights conventions apply and enforce strictly by states, government, and other institutions to heal the human society of the ills that has turned into a plague.

CONCLUSIONS

This book has taken a critical look at the different kinds of inequality affecting our society and its consequential formatting of tension, violence, and conflict. In fact, it does not cover all the points that address these issues but is pertinent that we see how this has affected and continued to affect our society. Inequality is against human rights laws and human dignity and therefore needs to be addressed to reduce the degree of how unequal we are in our world. The earlier societies that built on communalism proved that equal society is possible to a certain degree.

As Plutarch the Greek philosopher said, 'inequality is an imbalance between the rich and poor and that is the oldest and most fatal ailments of all Republics.' So have you ever asked yourself, how do I feel when others unequally treat me? This can offer each one of us an opportunity to think how to solve this problem of inequality.

Many schools of thoughts have pointed out how those who benefit from inequality favours it. George Bernard Shaw (1856–1950), a socialist, said, 'Always idiots are in favour of inequality of income; their only chance of eminence.' Pope John Paul II also said, 'Unequal states can be disastrous when it comes to application of "Free Trade", but the developed nations prefer a free trade based on unequal status.' Globalization should take into account the issue of unequal ways the developed countries deal with the developing nation, which at all times are victims of the rich countries.

From the fundamental standard of humanity, we have seen that people's 'Human Rights' are abused or violated because of the practice of different types of inequality. Inequality creates internal and external tension, violence, and conflict. When verbal, those in authority ignore agitations; there is the tendency that it takes the dimension of arms struggle and greater conflicts.

In Finland 1990, a group of nongovernmental experts offered a Declaration on minimum humanitarian standards. After studying the subcommission on Prevention of Discrimination and Protection of Minorities in 1991 and 1994, the declaration offered in Finland transmitted to United Nations Commission on Human Rights. Following the workshop in Cape Town in September 1996, the Commission on Human Rights requested the Secretary-General of the UN Economic and Social Council to prepare an analytical report on the issue of the fundamental standard of humanity. The unequal treatment and imbalance in all areas of human society are the roots causes of tension, violence, and conflict around the world. It is quite appalling that governments around the globe, after adopting laws and conventions against all forms of inequalities, are the same people who encourage and practice inequality for their benefit and that of their race, gender, ethnic, and social class. The benefit of inequality to those who sanction it has made this disease incurable. The international organizations, such as the UN, Amnesty International, UNESCO, UNICEF, International Criminal Court (ICC), and states have obligation to enforce their commitment to these laws without fear or favour. The ideal and principle of equity in law have to be interpreted without allowing some to be above the law.

Those states and enterprises that run guns and weapons across the borders of the developing nations, encouraging and aiding conflicts that destroy lives and properties should be duly prosecuted. Also, the hypocrisy of the five permanent member-states of the UN and their close allies should be exposed, since they adopted and signed all conventions and treaties, and at same time broke the role.

However, from all indications, all forms of inequalities have originated from the five big powers during the colonial era, and have even continued with them both internally and externally. Many suffering today under inequality can in one way or another trace it back to the big power brokers and Western allies. The elimination or reduction of inequality practiced, aided, and supported by all who favour it, whether it be religious, racial, ethnic, social, wealth and income, and disparity between the rich and the poor, must be an important agenda for the community of nations to work on collectively with all fairness to bring inequality to an end.

When you look at the Millennium Development Goals (MDGs), you would believe that if these goals are realized in the near future, we can reduce the plague of inequalities in our society. At the Millennium Summit held in September 2000, a good idea was born but until this day, we are still dragging our feet to reach the goals. This summit was one of the largest gatherings of world leaders in history. In this UN summit, they adopted the Millennium declaration committing their nations to new global partnership to reduce extreme poverty and setting out a series of time-bound targets, with deadline of 2015 to realize its goals. In fact in the 2009 Millennium Development Report released earlier in 2009, UN Secretary-General Ban Ki Moon said that progress has been made in MDG's effort and much success on which to build, but we are moving too slowly to meet our goals. He also said that 'Time is short, we must seize the moment to act responsibly and decisively for the common good.' Today, I join Ban Ki Moon in saying the same thing—let us act responsibly, decisively, and collectively to rid our society of inequalities and its inherent tension for a better tomorrow.

This book calls all of us to question in morality, fairness, and justice. We all are part of humanity, individually and collectively, and are therefore required to contribute our quota in making the world a better place for you and me and the entire human race. As the late Michael Jackson said, 'Let us speak out in all honesty and act in all fairness against inequality and its causes and its associated consequences wherever it exists, irrespective of religion, race, social and political affiliation. Say no to evil and resist it and it will not continue to thrive.'

REFERENCES

The Civil rights movement	Steven Kasher 1954-1968
Women in civil rights movement	Barbara Woods 1941-1965
The affluence society	John K. Galbraith
Implementing economic, social and cultural rights	Philip Alston
Dignity and human rights	Berna Klein Godelijk 2002
Racism: Wikipedia.Org	
Many faces of Gender inequality	Prof Amartya Sen
Caste and social problems	Hinduonnet.com/fline.
World Health Organization, Hand book of	
Human Nutrition Geneva (WHO), 1974.	
Women's Role in development	Ester Boserup
How does mother's schooling affects	
Family health, household sanitation, etc.	
Journal of econometrics, 1987	
Hidden penalties of gender inequality	
Siddiq Osmani and Amartya Sen,2001	
New African magazine October 2008	
The lives of American suffragists	Baker Jean H. Sisters
Women suffrage.htm.	
Winning of women suffrage	DuBois Ellen 1997
http//en.wikipedia.org/wiki.castesystem	
women not allowed to vote	
www.wisegeek.com.	
Racism changing stand point	R.G. Grant and Saskia de Groot
Religion and economy	Barbara Harris white, 2003
Equal treatment	Hartman and Eva, Cremers, 2005
The struggle for civil Rights in Mississippi	John Ditmer
The growth of civilization	W. I. Perry, 1937

The New Industrial State	John GR. Galbraith, 1967
Implementing Economic, Social, and Cultural Rights	Philip Alston
Dignity and Human Rights	Berns Klein Godelijk
The Growth of Civilzation	W. J. Perry, 1937
Racism	Wikipedia.org
The Many Faces of Gender Inequality	Prof. AMARTYA Sen.
Caste and Social Problems	Hindusconnect.com
Religion And Economy	Barbar Harris White, 2003
The Struggle for Civil Rights in Mississippi	John Ditner
Civil Rights Movement, 1954–68, Author Biographic History	Steven Kasher
Social Inequality, Forms, Causes, and Consequenses	Hurst (2006)
Inequality and Stratification, Class, Gender, and Race	Rothner R. A., 2005
Winning of Women Suffrage	Dubois Ellen, 1977
Realities of Gender Inequalities	Siddig Omanni and A. Martya Sen.
Women Not Allowed to Vote	www.wisegeek.com
Economic Inequality in the United States	Obsberg Lars, New York, Me Nc 1 1984
Wiki Castes System	Wikipedia.org
Racism Changing Standpoint	R.G. Grant and Saskia de Groot
Civil Rights Movement	New York, Greenwood Press, P.56.
The Battle of Selma (report)	Warren Hinkle and David Welsh, June 4, 1965, p. 36
Hidden Realities of Gender Inequalities 2001.	Siddiq Osmanni And Amartya Sen
Handbook of Human Nutrition	World Health Organization
Women's Role in Development	Geneva WHO, 1974
Women in Civil Rights Movement	Barbara Woods, 1941–1945
How Does Mother's Schooling Affects Family, Health, Household, Sanitation, etc.	Journal of Economists, 1987
The Lives of American Suffragists	Baker, Jean H. Sisters
Equal Treatment	Hartmenand Eva, Cremers 2005

www.ingramcontent.com/pod-product-compliance
Lightning Source LLC
Chambersburg PA
CBHW020508290526
45786CB00002B/518